Adventures in Phonics

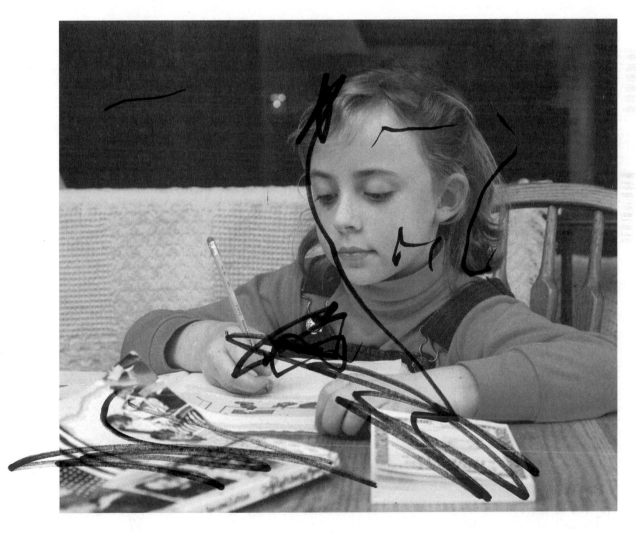

Level C

A publication of
Christian Liberty Press
502 West Euclid Avenue
Arlington Heights, Illinois 60004
www.christianlibertypress.com

Written by Florence M. Lindstrom
Layout and editing by Edward J. Shewan
Copyediting by Belit M. Shewan and Diane Olson
Cover design by Bob Fine

ISBN 1-930092-80-6

Printed in the United States of America

For the Teacher

The primary goal of phonics instruction is to help the student become a strong reader by teaching him the *sounds* made by individual letters and combinations of letters. This will enable him to sound out an unlimited number of words. Emphasis should be placed upon teaching the *sound* of each letter and *not* its name. Only the *sounds* of the letters help us read words. Once your student understands the basic rules of phonics, the world of reading will open up to him. This will also enable him to be a good speller.

It is important for teachers to follow the instructions located in this **Teacher's Manual** as a preparation for the daily lessons in *Adventures in Phonics Level C*. A home school teacher is able to have his student read drills from this **Teacher's Manual**. Keep in mind that each student learns at a different rate of speed depending on his previous schooling, his maturity, and the difficulty of the lesson. If your student has completed *Adventures in Phonics Level B*, many of the lessons will serve as a review and reinforcement of that workbook. If *Adventures in Phonics Level C*, however, is the first exposure to learning the sounds of the letters and to reading, the student may need extra drill and review. This workbook may be helpful to the older student who has not had a phonics background during his younger years of school. Many new words will be taught. **Spend as much time as you feel necessary to help your student understand each lesson.**

In the student's workbook, the pages have been perforated so that they can easily be removed to help the student in completing his work. All the student's work should be carefully saved for review purposes. The instructor may choose to have his student do the work in the workbook, keeping it all together.

As new work is introduced, it is recommended that the teacher go over the entire lesson with the student, making sure he understands the directions and knows what the pictures represent. The student should also give the answers orally; this is not a test, but a time of teaching and learning. Finally, he should neatly complete the page independently. The teacher should correct the student's work as soon as possible and have him rework any errors he makes. Before beginning the next lesson, a short time should be spent discussing the previous lesson.

The two most important attributes of a phonics teacher are loving patience and caring perseverance. May the Lord grant you, the instructor, an abundant supply of both.

Florence Lindstrom

Christian Liberty Academy

Arlington Heights, IL

Page 1

Purpose

To review the sounds of consonants and vowels through reading words.

To review printing the capitals and small letters of the alphabet.

Lesson

Listen as your student says the sounds of each letter in the alphabet. Discuss the purpose of capitals such as writing the name of a person (Adam), or place (Garden of Eden), or beginning sentences, etc.

<u>T</u>his is the day that the <u>L</u>ord has made.

<u>W</u>e will rejoice and be glad in it.

Discuss the directions and go over the lesson as the student gives the answers orally. Give help as needed. Have him complete the lesson independently, stressing neatness as he begins this new workbook, and as he does the work on each page.

Check the lesson soon after it has been completed, and have the student make any corrections.

Page 2

Purpose

To give practice in reading short vowel **a** words.

To introduce two-syllable words with a short vowel **a** sound in the first syllable. These words usually follow **Rules 5** or **6** for syllabication which are introduced later in the workbook (pages 106 and 110).

Lesson

Ask the student to read the words on **Chart 1** (found on page 181 in the workbook), taking notice of consonant blends that may be at the beginning or ending of the words.

Help the student read the following two-syllable words with a short vowel **a** in the first syllable. Tell him that each part of a word (i.e., a *syllable*) has a vowel sound.

batter   grandma   napkin

cactus   habit   panther

daddy   jacket   radish

fabric   ladder   salad

Discuss the directions and go over the lesson as the student gives the answers orally. Give help as needed. Have him complete the lesson independently, stressing neatness in all the work.

Page 3

Purpose

To give additional practice in reading and printing short vowel **a** words.

To become more familiar with two-syllable words with a short vowel **a** sound in the first syllable.

Lesson

Have a quick review of the previous lesson with the student. It would be good to have him read the words on **Chart 1** again.

Help the student read these two-syllable words with a short vowel **a** in the first syllable. Give encouragement and compliments whenever possible.

banner   hammer   raccoon

candy   master   ravel

famine   panel   sandal

gallop   pantry   tablet

Discuss the directions and go over the lesson as the student gives the answers orally. Give help as needed. Have him complete the lesson independently, stressing neatness in all the work.

Note: In the first two exercises on page 3 of the student workbook, the answer *cab* could also be *taxi*. In addition, the answers *rabbit* and *rascal* could be used interchangeably in the last sentence on the worksheet.

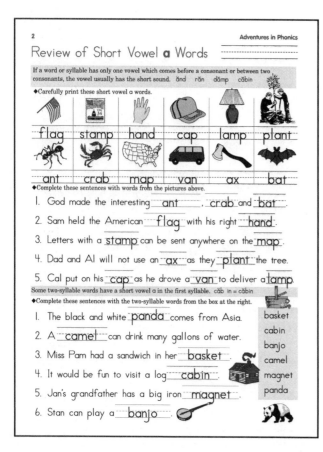

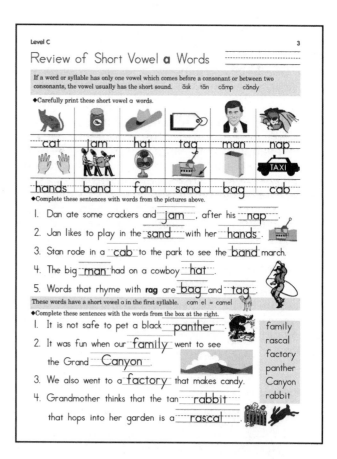

Page 4

Purpose

To give practice in reading and printing short vowel **e** words.

To introduce two-syllable words with a short vowel **e** sound in the first syllable.

Lesson

Ask the student to read the words on **Chart 2** (found on page 181 in the workbook), taking notice of consonant blends that may be at the beginning or ending of the words.

Help the student read the following two-syllable words with a short vowel **e** in the first syllable. Give encouragement whenever possible.

beggar	lesson	pencil
devil	medal	petal
dessert	menu	rebel
hello	neglect	second

Discuss the directions and go over the lesson as the student gives the answers orally. Give help as needed. Have him complete the lesson independently, stressing neatness in all the work.

Page 5

Purpose

To give additional practice in reading and printing short vowel **e** words.

To review words spelled with the digraph **ea** that makes the short **e** vowel sound.

Lesson

Have a quick review of the previous lesson with the student. Listen as the student practices reading the list of digraph **ea** words on **Chart 12** (found on page 183 in the workbook). Spend as much time as necessary. Give encouragement and compliments.

Listen as he reads these words with the digraph **ea**:

feather	thread	jealous
sweater	heaven	wealth
bread	heavy	pleasant
head	measure	instead

Discuss the directions and go over the lesson as the student gives the answers orally. Give help as needed. Have him complete the lesson independently, stressing neatness in all the work.

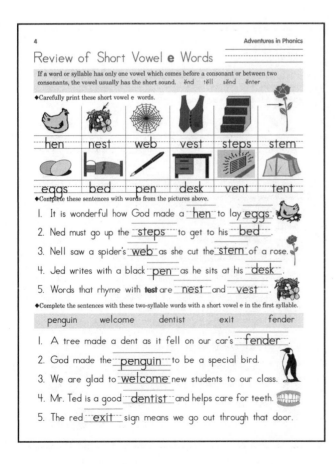

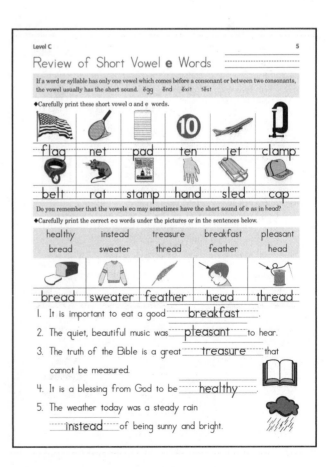

Page 6

Purpose

To give practice in reading and printing short vowel **i** words.

To introduce two-syllable words with a short vowel **i** sound in the first syllable.

Lesson

Have the student practice reading the list of short vowel **i** words on **Chart 3** (found on page 181 in the workbook).

Help your student read the following two-syllable words with a short vowel **i** in the first syllable. Encourage and compliment him whenever possible.

hiccup	dipper	linen
pillow	fifteen	lily
clipper	finger	mission
dislike	kingdom	mixture

Discuss the directions and go over the lesson as the student gives the answers orally. Give help as needed. Stress neatness as he completes the lesson independently.

Page 7

Purpose

To give additional practice in reading and printing short vowel **i** words.

To become more familiar with two-syllable words having a short vowel **i** sound in the first syllable.

Lesson

Go over the previous lesson with the student. Again have the student practice reading the list of short vowel **i** words on **Chart 3**.

Listen and help when necessary as your student reads the following two-syllable words with a short vowel **i** in the first syllable. Give encouragement.

million	fiction	limit
clinic	figure	lily
dictate	kitten	kingdom
discount	minnow	bitter

Listen as your student reads the words in the lesson and orally answers the sentences before he does the work independently.

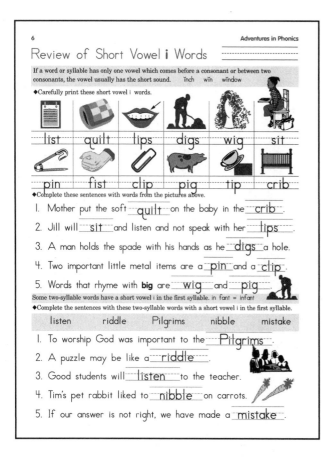

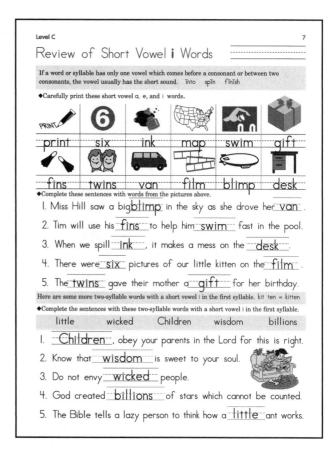

Page 8

Purpose

To give practice in reading and printing short vowel **o** words.

To introduce two-syllable words with a short vowel **o** sound in the first syllable.

Lesson

Have the student practice reading the list of short vowel o words on **Chart 4** (found on page 181 in the workbook). Listen patiently as you encourage and commend.

Help your student read the following two-syllable words with a short vowel **o** in the first syllable. Be encouraging.

bottom	gossip	model
bonnet	hollow	pocket
comma	jolly	robber
conduct	lobby	rocket

Listen while your student gives the answers to the lesson orally before he completes it independently.

Page 9

Purpose

To give practice in reading and printing short vowel **a**, **e**, **i**, and **o** words.

To learn to read more two-syllable words with a short vowel **a**, **e**, **i**, or **o** sound in the first syllable.

Lesson

Take a quick review of the previous lesson with the student. Have the student practice reading from some of the lists of short vowel **a**, **e**, **i**, and **o** words on **Charts 1–4** (found on page 181 in the workbook).

Help your student read the following two-syllable words with a short vowel **a**, **e**, **i**, or **o** sound in the first syllable. Encourage and commend.

blossom	gospel	monarch
fender	finger	penguin
bother	jonquil	ponder
handle	panda	banner

Listen while your student gives the answers to the lesson orally before he completes it independently.

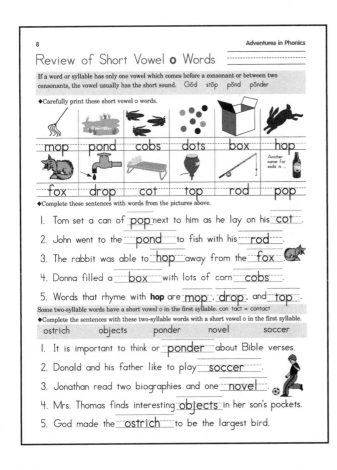

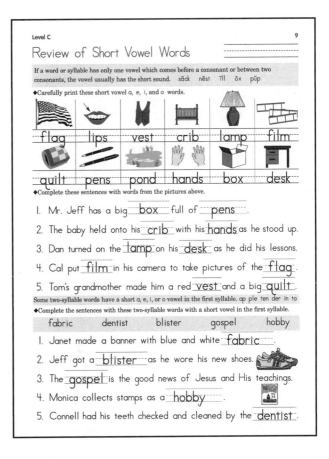

Page 10

Purpose

To give practice in reading and printing short vowel **u** words.

To learn to read two-syllable words with a short vowel **u** sound in the first syllable.

Lesson

Have the student practice reading the list of short vowel **u** words on **Chart 5** (found on page 182 in the workbook).

Read with your student the following two-syllable words with a short vowel **u** in the first syllable. Give encouragement.

bucket	fungus	humming
butter	funny	justice
clumsy	gutter	lumber
custom	husky	slumber

Listen while your student gives the answers to the lesson orally before completing it independently.

Page 11

Purpose

To review words spelled with **o** which have the short vowel sound of **u**.

Lesson

Spend as much time as necessary as your student reads **Chart 6** (found on page 182 in the workbook) with words having the short vowel **u** sound made by the vowel **o**. Many of these words will be read for the first time. Study the list until you feel he knows the words well.

Listen while your student gives the answers to the lesson orally before completing it independently.

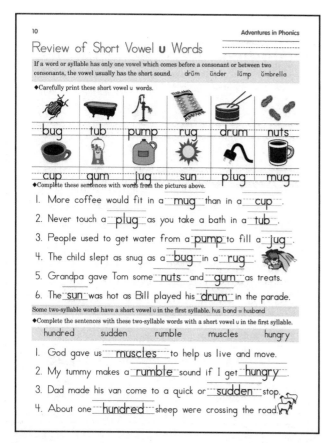

10   Adventures in Phonics

Review of Short Vowel **u** Words

If a word or syllable has only one vowel which comes before a consonant or between two consonants, the vowel usually has the short sound.   drŭm   ŭnder   lŭmp   ŭmbrella

◆Carefully print these short vowel u words.

bug	tub	pump	rug	drum	nuts
cup	gum	jug	sun	plug	mug

◆Complete these sentences with words from the pictures above.

1. More coffee would fit in a __mug__ than in a __cup__.
2. Never touch a __plug__ as you take a bath in a __tub__.
3. People used to get water from a __pump__ to fill a __jug__.
4. The child slept as snug as a __bug__ in a __rug__.
5. Grandpa gave Tom some __nuts__ and __gum__ as treats.
6. The __sun__ was hot as Bill played his __drum__ in the parade.

Some two-syllable words have a short vowel u in the first syllable. hus band = husband

◆Complete the sentences with these two-syllable words with a short vowel u in the first syllable.

hundred	sudden	rumble	muscles	hungry

1. God gave us __muscles__ to help us live and move.
2. My tummy makes a __rumble__ sound if I get __hungry__.
3. Dad made his van come to a quick or __sudden__ stop.
4. About one __hundred__ sheep were crossing the road.

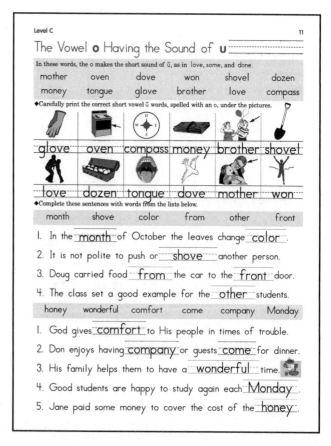

Level C   11

The Vowel **o** Having the Sound of **u**

In these words, the o makes the short sound of ŭ, as in love, some, and done.

mother	oven	dove	won	shovel	dozen
money	tongue	glove	brother	love	compass

◆Carefully print the correct short vowel ŭ words, spelled with an o, under the pictures.

glove	oven	compass	money	brother	shovel
love	dozen	tongue	dove	mother	won

◆Complete these sentences with words from the lists below.

month	shove	color	from	other	front

1. In the __month__ of October the leaves change __color__.
2. It is not polite to push or __shove__ another person.
3. Doug carried food __from__ the car to the __front__ door.
4. The class set a good example for the __other__ students.

honey	wonderful	comfort	come	company	Monday

1. God gives __comfort__ to His people in times of trouble.
2. Don enjoys having __company__ or guests __come__ for dinner.
3. His family helps them to have a __wonderful__ time.
4. Good students are happy to study again each __Monday__.
5. Jane paid some money to cover the cost of the __honey__.

Page 12

Purpose

To review short vowel words which end with **ff**, **ll**, **ss**, **zz**, and **ck**.

Lesson

Have your student read **Chart 7** (found on page 182 in the workbook) with short vowel words ending with **ck**. The consonant digraph **ck**, which can never be divided, is said with the short vowel. Review the rule regarding the ending consonants **ff**, **ll**, **ss**, and **zz** as it is found at the top of the lesson. Listen to him read the following two-syllable, short vowel words that have **ck** in the first syllable.

jacket	knuckle	tickle
packet	freckle	locket
racket	speckle	pocket
buckle	pickle	rocket

Listen as your student says all the names of the pictures and words on the lists. Have him give the answers to the lesson orally, before he completes it independently.

Note: The answer under the picture of a brick wall in the middle of page 12 may be either *brick* or *bricks*.

Page 13

Purpose

To review short vowel words which end with **ff**, **ll**, **ss**, **zz**, and **ck**.

Lesson

Have your student again read **Chart 7** with short vowel words ending with **ck**.

Carefully study the following words. When a word has a short vowel sound, the letters **ff**, **ll**, **ss**, **zz**, and **ck** are used. In long vowel words these letters are not doubled.

fill	file	lack	lake
mill	mile	fuss	fuse
well	wheel	snack	snake
whiff	wife	bass	base

Discuss the entire lesson with your student. Have him give the answers orally before he completes it independently.

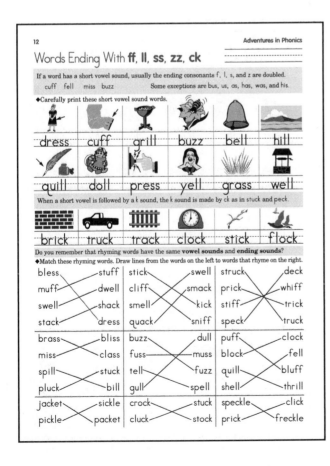

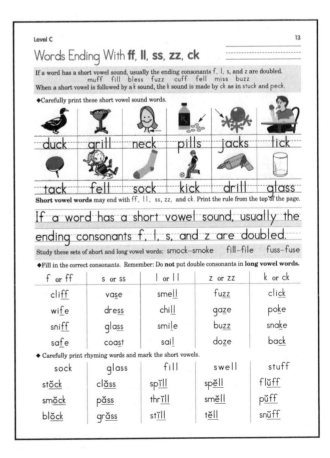

Page 14

Purpose
To review short vowel words ending with the sounds **ng** and **nk**.

Lesson
Review the previous lesson with the student. Listen closely to hear if your student correctly pronounces the words on **Chart 23** (found on page 186 in the workbook). The letter **g** should not make its regular sound as in *get*. Spend as much time as necessary for him to learn these words well.

Compare the sound **ng** makes in these words:

sing single shingle
tang tangle

Teach the entire lesson as your student gives the answers orally before he completes it independently.

Page 15

Purpose
To review more short vowel words ending with the sounds **ng** or **nk**.

To review compound words.

Lesson
Review the previous lesson with the student. Print the following words on the board or a paper and listen closely to hear if your student says them correctly; the letter **g** should **not** make its regular sound as in *get*.

think	sank	wink
thing	sang	wing
sink	brink	clank
sing	bring	clang

Be sure your student understands all of the directions on the page and gives the answers to the lesson orally before he completes it independently.

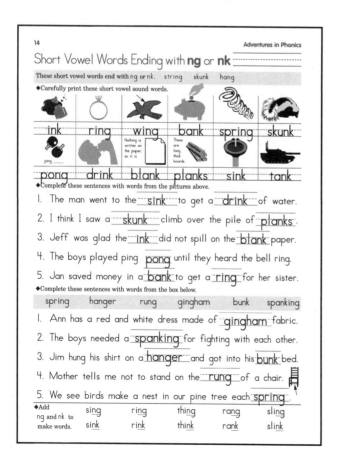

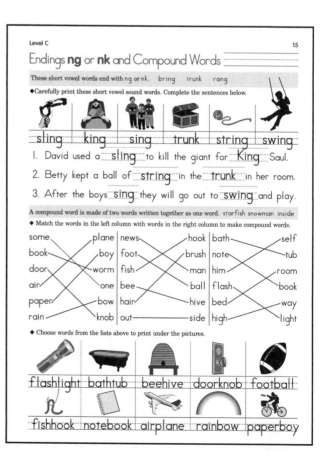

Page 16

Purpose

To review words with digraphs **ch**, **sh**, **th**, and **wh**.

Lesson

Print the following words on the board or a paper and listen closely to hear if your student says them correctly. The digraph **th** has two sounds:

the	that	them	this
thin	bath	thick	with
whip	when	which	wheel
shelf	rush	shock	smash
much	check	lunch	chin

Have the student practice reading digraph **ch**, **sh**, **th**, and **wh** words on **Chart 8** (found on page 182 in the workbook).

Listen as your student gives the answers to the lesson orally before completing it by himself.

Page 17

Purpose

To review words with the digraphs **gh** and **ph** which make the sound of **f** as in *pheasant*.

Lesson

Review the previous lesson. Listen and help as **Chart 9** (found on page 183 in the workbook) is read. Print these words on the board or a paper, or have them read from this key. Mention that **gh** is sometimes silent. It will be taught in other lessons. Listen as these words are read.

nephew	alphabet
laugh	dolphin
cough	phrase
pamphlet	hyphen
tough	digraphs
telephone	pharmacy
rough	elephant

Listen as your student gives the answers to the lesson orally before completing it by himself.

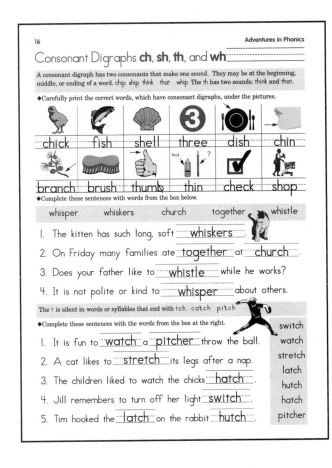

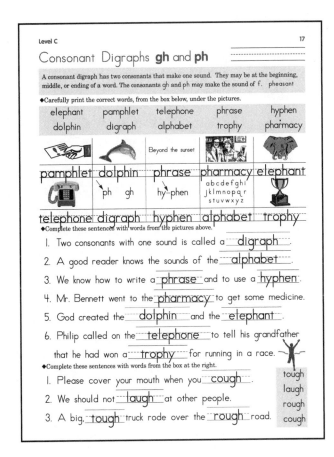

Page 18

Purpose

To reinforce words with the long vowel sound of **a**.

Lesson

Be familiar with the directions on the workbook page as you discuss the difference between short vowel and long vowel sounds. By now the student should know the main five vowels: **a**, **e**, **i**, **o**, and **u**. Say the long vowel rule several times, having your student repeat it after you. Discuss and study the following words with him:

past	paste	cap	cape
back	bake	tap	tape
pan	pane	hat	hate
bran	brain	bath	bathe
slat	slate	mad	maid

Study the long vowel **a** words on **Chart 10** (found on page 183 in the workbook).

Go over the spelling of each picture word, and listen as the student gives the answers to the lesson orally before he completes it independently.

Page 19

Purpose

To reinforce words with the long vowel sound of **a**.

To review digraphs and consonant blends.

Lesson

Go over the previous lesson with the student. Read the directions on the workbook page as you review the difference between a short vowel sound and a long vowel sound. Does the student remember the long vowel rule? Have it repeated as you say it several times. Study these words with your student.

tap	tape	ran	rain
mat	mate	man	main
pad	paid	rat	rate
pal	pail	bat	bait

Review the long vowel **a** words on **Chart 10**.

Listen as he gives the answers to the lesson orally before he completes it independently.

Some lessons may take a longer time than others, but it is important that the student understands what is being taught. It is better that a second day be spent on a lesson, if there is uncertainty, than to go on and become more confused.

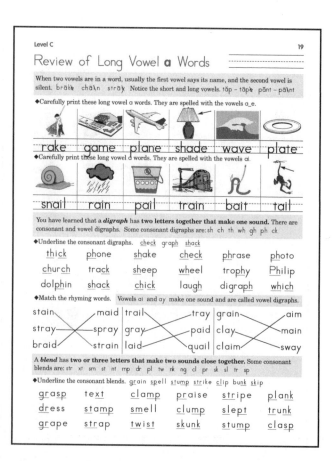

Page 20

Purpose
To teach the long vowel sound of **e**.

Lesson
Review the difference between a short vowel sound and a long vowel sound. Say the long vowel rule several times, having it repeated after you. Read the following words with your student:

men	mean	fell	feel
bed	bead	met	meat
sell	seal	stem	steam
step	steep	set	seat

Study the long vowel **e** words on **Chart 11** (found on page 183 in the workbook).

Listen and help as your student studies and reads all of the words on the page. Let him give the answers to the lesson orally before he completes it independently.

Page 21

Purpose
To teach the long vowel sound of **e**.

Lesson
Review the previous lesson with the student. Read the directions on the workbook page as you explain the difference between a short vowel sound and a long vowel sound. Discuss the long vowel rule, asking the student to tell it to you. Read the following words with your student:

ten	teen	net	neat
red	read	hell	heal
Ben	bean	pep	peep
den	dean	peck	peak

Study the long vowel **e** words on **Chart 11**.

Discuss the sound of long **a** that **ea** makes in a few words like these:

break great steak

Listen as your student reads all of the words on the lists and gives the answers to the lesson orally before he completes it independently.

---

20   Adventures in Phonics

Review of Long Vowel **e** Words

When two vowels are in a word, usually the first vowel says its name, and the second vowel is silent. lēₐf bēₑ kēy̆ Notice the short and long vowels. lĕd – lēₐd sĕt – sēₐt

◆Carefully print these long vowel e words. They are spelled with the vowels **ee**.

jeep	sleep	feet	sheep	peel	three
heel	teeth	bee	tree	beet	deer

◆Carefully print these long vowel e words. They are spelled with the vowels **ea**.

seal	leaf	ear	peas	tears	team

◆Complete these sentences with the two-syllable, long vowel e words from the box at the right.

1. I did not feel well when I had the __measles__.
2. It was not easy for the __feeble__ man to walk.
3. Jean saw a __weasel__ nibble on a __peanut__.
4. Mother will teach Steve how to use a thread and __needle__ to sew on a button.

| peanut |
| weasel |
| feeble |
| measles |
| needle |

◆Complete these sentences with the long vowel e words from the box at the right.

1. God created the __peacock__ and __beetle__.
2. God also made each __season__ of the year.
3. He gave us the ability to think and __reason__.
4. The Lord Jesus is our best __teacher__.

| peacock |
| reason |
| season |
| teacher |
| beetle |

Level C   **21**

Review of Long Vowel **e** Words

If two vowels are in a word, usually the first vowel says its name, and the second vowel is silent. sēₐl clēₐr whēₐt An e has a long sound at the end of these words. hē wē shē mē bē

◆Carefully print these long vowel e words. They are spelled with the vowels **ea**.

teach	steam	wheat	flea	cream	meal

◆Complete these sentences with the short and long vowel e words at the right.

1. The __men__ are not __mean__ as they catch a beaver.
2. I will be careful as I __step__ down a __steep__ cliff.
3. It would not __feel__ good if I __fell__ down.
4. Glen will __meet__ a man he has not __met__ before.
5. How much will a zoo get to __sell__ a __seat__?

| mean |
| men |
| steep |
| step |
| feel |
| fell |
| meet |
| met |
| seal |
| sell |

◆Complete these sentences with the long vowel e words from the box at the right.

1. Cal's computer __screen__ needs to be cleaned.
2. Gene seeks to __greet__ new people at church.
3. I have __greed__ if I am first to __reach__ for food.
4. Mr. Green got cream on his left __sleeve__.
5. It was peaceful to watch a beaver near a __stream__.
6. As we are kind to others we __cheer__ them.

| reach |
| greet |
| stream |
| screen |
| cheer |
| greed |
| sleeve |

◆Complete these sentences with the long vowel a words at the right. They are spelled with the vowels ea.

1. Our __great__ God created the heavens and the earth.
2. We heard the branch __break__ during the storm.

| break |
| great |

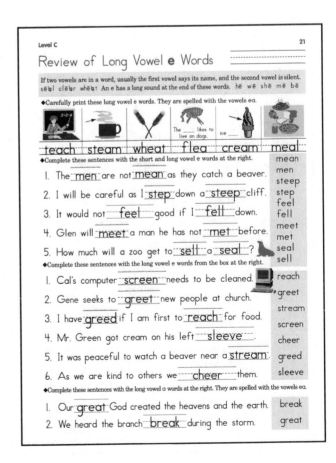

Page 22

Purpose
To review and reinforce the long vowel sound of **i**.

Lesson
Be familiar with the directions on the workbook page as you review the difference between a short vowel sound and a long vowel sound. See if your student can explain the long vowel rule. Read the following words with your student:

slid	slide	bit	bite
rip	ripe	pin	pine
kit	kite	win	wine
hid	hide	rid	ride

Spend as much time as necessary as you study the long vowel **i** words on **Chart 13** (found on page 184 in the workbook).

Listen as your student reads all of the words on the lists and gives the answers to the lesson orally before he completes it independently.

Page 23

Purpose
To reinforce words with the long vowel sound of **i**.

Lesson
Have a quick review of the previous lesson with the student. Review the directions on the workbook page as you talk about the difference between a short vowel sound and a long vowel sound. Teach that **y** is a vowel at the end of these words, and has the long vowel sound of **i**. Also review the long vowel sound of an **i** in words ending with **ld**, **nd**, or silent **gh**. Read the following words with your student:

my	why	bind	fight
shy	mild	blind	light
sky	child	find	right
spy	wild	grind	sight

Study the long vowel **i** words on **Chart 17** (found on page 185 in the workbook), and review **Chart 13** if the student still needs a little extra study.

Listen as your student gives the answers to the lesson orally before he completes it independently.

---

22   Adventures in Phonics

Review of Long Vowel i Words

When two vowels are in a word, usually the first vowel says its name, and the second vowel is silent. dive tie Notice the short and long vowels. mill - mile Tim - time

◆Carefully print these long vowel i words. They are spelled with the vowels i_e.

vine	smile	tire	bride	pile	ride
dime	pipe	fire	nine	line	hive

◆Complete these sentences with the compound words from the box at the right. fire+man = fireman

1. Mike gave his father a ___necktie___ for his birthday.
2. Men put a ___pipeline___ for water in our yard.
3. Kim looked for each ___milepost___ as she travelled.
4. Could we ride a bike ___nineteen___ miles in a day?
5. A ___pineapple___ is a juicy, tropical fruit.
6. Two men used a ___lifeboat___ to rescue the sailor.
7. The boys rode on the ___sidewalk___ with their skates.

pipeline
sidewalk
nineteen
lifeboat
necktie
milepost
pineapple

◆Fill in the blanks. Think about the short and long vowel sounds in the words.

1. The light was ___dim___ so Tim did not see the ___dime___.
2. Kim will use the ___kit___ to make a ___kite___.
3. It was fun as Mike ___slid___ down the ___slide___.
4. It is ___time___ for ___Tim___ to do his homework.

dime
dim
kite
kit
slide
slid
time
Tim

Level C   23

Review of Long Vowel i Words

When two vowels are in a word, usually the first vowel says its name, and the second vowel is silent. bite pie Y is a vowel if it is at the end of a word. In these words it has a long i sound. sky

◆Carefully print these long vowel i words. The y makes the long i sound.

fly	cry	sky	fry	dry	shy

bashful

◆Add y to complete these words.

shy	sly	pry	my	why	try	by	spy

◆Add ie.

lie	tie	pie	lied	die	tied

Usually the vowel i is short when it is alone in a word. In these words the vowel is long because it is followed by ld, nd, or gh. The consonants gh are silent. mild mind might

◆Complete these sentences with the long vowel i words from the box at the right.

1. The kind ___child___ helped to lead the ___blind___ man.
2. It is not ___right___ if children ___fight___ with each other.
3. One dark ___night___ we saw a ___wild___ bear.

wild
night
fight
blind
child
right

◆Complete these sentences with the words from the box at the right.

1. It ran from the ___bright___ light of our ___flashlight___.
2. Grandfather had to look ___behind___ the pine tree to ___find___ his newspaper.
3. He had to ___remind___ Tim that he ___might___ try to throw it right on his sidewalk.

behind
remind
might
find
flashlight
bright

◆Complete these words by filling in igh. The consonants gh are silent.

high	sigh	nigh	sight	bright	light
right	fight	fright	might	flight	slight

Page 24

Purpose
To reinforce words with the long vowel sound of **o**.

Lesson
Say the long vowel rule several times, having your student repeat it after you say it. Apply this rule by studying the following words:

not	note	cot	coat
rob	robe	rod	road
tot	tote	got	goat
hop	hope	sock	soak

Does your student remember the rule that says there is usually only *one* vowel in short vowel words?

Spend as much time as necessary as you study the long vowel **o** words on **Chart 14** (found on page 184 in the workbook).

Study **Chart 16** (found on page 184 in the workbook) which has words with one vowel at the end of them.

Listen and help as your student gives the answers to the lesson orally before he completes it independently.

Page 25

Purpose
To review words ending with the long vowel sound of **o**.

Lesson
Go over the previous lesson with the student. Discuss the long vowel rule, asking the student to say it to you. Review the long vowel sound of **o** in the following words that end with **ld**, **st**, **th**, **ll**, or **lt**.

fold	post	roll	bolt
scold	most	stroll	colt
told	both	scroll	jolt

Study **Chart 18** (found on page 185 in the workbook), and review **Chart 14** if the student needs extra study. For a little change, take turns reading; you read one word and your student read the next word, etc.

Listen as your student goes over the entire lesson and gives the answers to the lesson orally before he completes it independently.

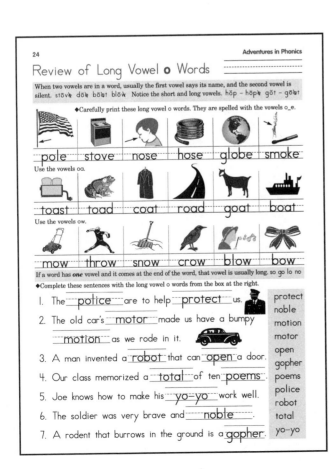

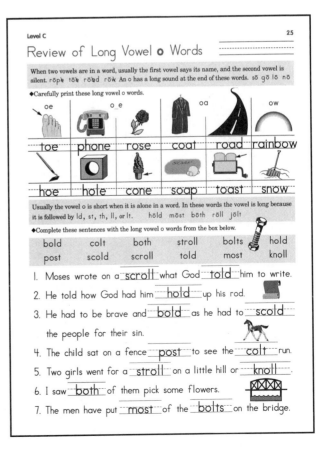

Page 26

Purpose

To review and reinforce the long vowel **u** sound.

Lesson

Again review the difference between a short vowel sound and a long vowel sound. Say the long vowel rule several times, having your student repeat it after you say it. Does he remember the rule about having only *one* vowel in most short vowel words? Read the following words with your student:

tub	tube	new	screw
cut	cute	flew	stew
cub	cube	drew	threw

Study the long vowel **u** words on **Chart 15** (found on page 184 in the workbook).

Listen and help when necessary as your student gives the answers to the lesson orally before he completes it independently.

Page 27

Purpose

To reinforce words with the long vowel **u** sound.

To discuss words ending with the sound of **v** followed by a silent **e**.

Lesson

Review the previous lesson with the student. Review the long vowel rule, asking the student to say it to you.

Discuss the fact that words ending with the sound of **v**—like the following words—usually end with a silent **e**, even though the vowel is short.

give	have	glove	love
live	shove	dove	above

Review the long vowel **u** words on **Chart 15.**

Listen and help as your student answers the lesson orally before he completes it independently.

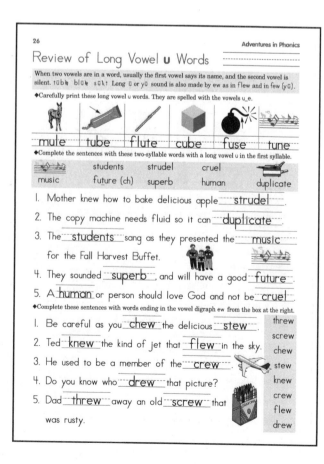

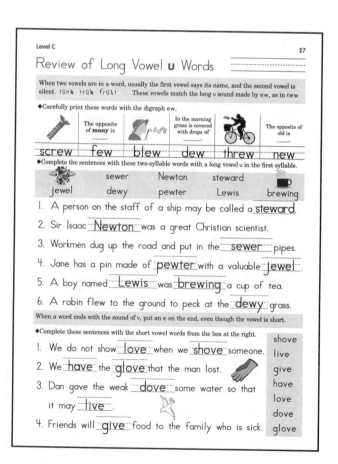

Page 28

Purpose

To review words that have the **hard** and **soft** sounds of **c**.

Lesson

Explain the rules about the hard and soft sounds of **c** as they appear at the top of the lesson. It is important to be familiar with these words through review and drill. The student will have a better understanding of why our alphabet includes these two letters (**c** and **k**) by studying the following words:

lake	lace	spike	spice
brake	brace	Mike	mice
pike	pice*	dike	dice
fake	face	like	lice
rake	race	spake	space

*A *pice* (pīs), or *paisa* (pī′ sá), is a unit of money used in India, Nepal, and Pakistan; it is equal to $\frac{1}{100}$ of a rupee.

Ask your student to read the words on **Chart 28** (found on page 188 in the workbook), repeating them as many times as necessary to know them well.

Listen as your student reads and gives the answers to the lesson orally before he completes it independently.

Page 29

Purpose

To review words that have the **hard** and **soft** sounds of **c**.

Lesson

Quickly go over the previous lesson with the student. Does the student think he did neat printing?

Review the rules about the hard and soft sounds of **c** as they appear at the top of the lesson.

Listen as the student reads the following words and identifies whether the **c** has a *hard* (**k**) or *soft* (**s**) sound.

voice	cabin	brace	face
crack	lace	trace	space
grace	mice	spice	city
since	Joyce	lice	price
creek	pencil	brace	cake

Review words on **Chart 28**.

Go over the lesson with your student as he reads and gives the answers to the lesson orally before he completes it independently

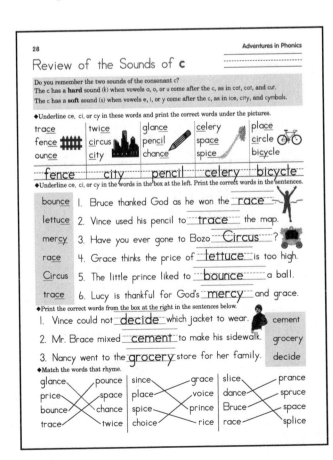

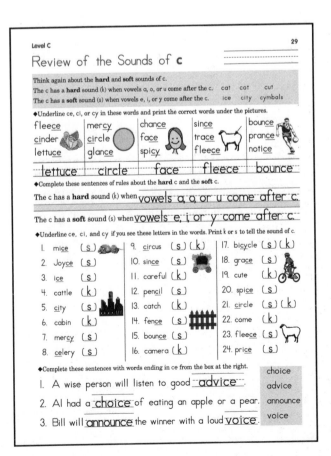

Page 30

Purpose

To review words that have the **hard** and **soft** sounds of **g**.

Lesson

Explain the rules about the hard and soft sounds of **g** as they appear at the top of the lesson. Have the student repeat several times the three vowels that change the **g**: **e**, **i**, or **y**.

Mention that there are several words that do not follow this rule: gift, get, gear, girl, give, etc.

Have your student think about the importance of the silent **e** as he says these sets of words:

rag — rage, stag — stage, hug — huge

Have him explain the sound of **g** in these words:

gopher   garage   Gary

gentle   giant   Egypt

Have your student read **Chart 29** (found on page 188 in the workbook).

Listen as he reads and gives the answers to the lesson orally before he completes it independently.

Check the work and have the student correct any errors as soon as he completes the lesson.

Page 31

Purpose

To review words that have the **hard** and **soft** sounds of **g**.

Lesson

Go over the previous lesson with the student. Review the rules about the hard and soft sounds of **g**. Again have the student repeat several times the three vowels that change the **g**: **e**, **i**, or **y**.

Listen as the student reads the following words and identifies whether the **g** has a *hard* (**g**) or *soft* (**j**) sound.

gym   wedge   guard

grape   hinge   goat

large   gypsy   guess

brag   ginger   gentle

Have him read the words on **Chart 29** again.

Go over the lesson with your student as he reads and gives the answers to the lesson orally before he completes it independently.

Check the work and have the student correct any errors as soon as he completes the lesson.

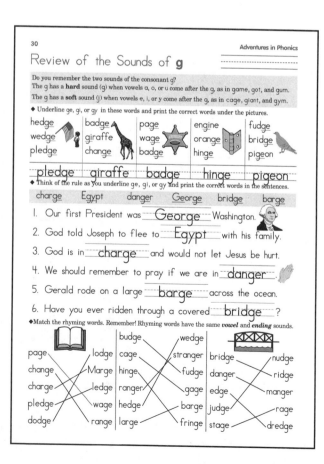

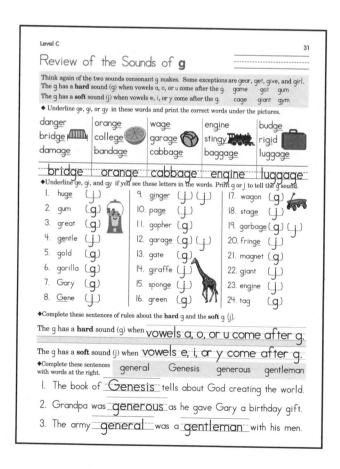

Page 32

Purpose

To review the sound of **oo** as in the word *zoo*.

Lesson

Listen as your student reads the words from **Chart 19** (found on page 185 in the workbook). It is important for him to know the words, so it is worth spending the time.

Talk about the work done on the previous lesson, and ask the student if he thinks he did neat work.

Listen as he reads all of the words on the lists and gives the answers to the lesson orally before he completes it independently.

Page 33

Purpose

To reinforce words with the sound of **oo** as in *food*.

Lesson

Review the previous lesson with the student. Listen as he reads the words from **Chart 19**. Spend as much time as needed for learning it well.

Review the four ways the sound of **oo** as in *food* may be spelled:

u_e as in *rule*, **ue** as in *true*,

ew as in *drew*, **oo** as in *food*

Listen as he reads all of the words on the lists and gives the answers to the lesson orally before he completes it independently.

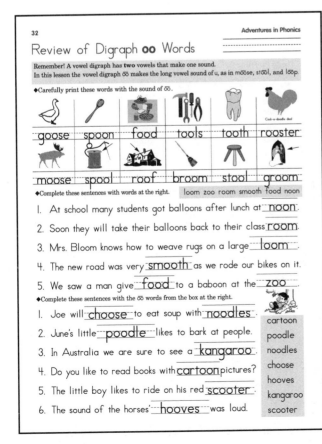

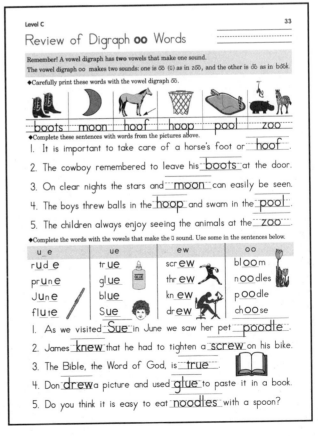

Page 34

Purpose

To reinforce words with the sound of **oo** as in *book*.

Lesson

Go over the previous lesson with the student.

Review the four ways the sound of **oo** as in *book* may be spelled:

oo as in book, **u** as in put,

o as in wolf, and **ou** as in should

Listen to him read the words from **Chart 20** (found on page 185 in the workbook). Spend as much time as needed for learning these words well.

Write the following words on the board and ask the student to mark the **oo** sounds correctly.

took   school   wool
food   brook   broom
shook   wood   football
bloom   cookies   loose
boost   balloon   stood

Listen as the student reads all of the words on the lists and gives the answers to the lesson orally before he completes it independently.

Page 35

Purpose

To review words with the sound of **oo** as in *foot*.

Lesson

Review the four ways this sound may be spelled:

oo as in good, **u** as in pull,

o as in wolf, and **ou** as in could

Listen to the student read the words from **Chart 20** again.

Listen as he reads all of the words on the lists and gives the answers to the lesson orally before he completes it independently.

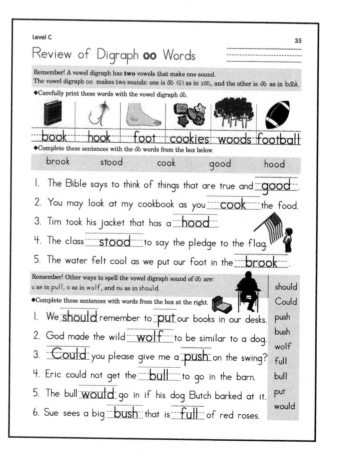

34   Adventures in Phonics

Review of Digraph oo Words

Remember! A vowel digraph has **two** vowels that make one sound.
The vowel digraph oo makes two sounds: one is o͞o (u͞) as in zo͞o, and the other is o͝o as in bo͝ok.

◆Carefully print these words with the vowel digraph o͝o.

wood   brook   wool   shook   crook   hood

◆Complete these sentences with the o͝o words from the box below.

| shook | hood | woodpecker | soot | crooked | footprints |

1. The man lifted the __hood__ of his car when it would not start.
2. Mr. Cook __shook__ off the __soot__ from the ashes of the fire.
3. The path in the woods was hilly and __crooked__
4. We saw a bird with a red head called a __woodpecker__
5. The tracks our feet make are called __footprints__

You may remember that there are other ways to spell the vowel digraph sound of o͝o. Study these sounds: u as in put, o as in wolf, and ou as in should.

◆Complete the words with the vowels that make the sound of o͝o.

u	o	ou	o͝o
bu__sh__	bu__ll__	w__o__lf	w__ou__ld	cr__oo__k	w__oo__l
pu__sh__	pu__ll__		c__ou__ld	sh__oo__k	t__oo__k
fu__ll__	__put__	w__o__lves	sh__ou__ld	st__oo__d	woodpile

◆Mark the correct sound of the vowel digraph oo (o͞o or o͝o) in each of these words.

look	troop	bloom	baboon	hood	cartoon
stool	wood	raccoon	wool	scoop	lagoon
school	roost	stood	book	balloon	boost
shook	crooked	soot		loose	choose

Level C   35

Review of Digraph oo Words

Remember! A vowel digraph has **two** vowels that make one sound.
The vowel digraph oo makes two sounds: one is o͞o (u͞) as in zo͞o, and the other is o͝o as in bo͝ok.

◆Carefully print these words with the vowel digraph o͝o.

book   hook   foot   cookies   woods   football

◆Complete these sentences with the o͝o words from the box below.

| brook | stood | cook | good | hood |

1. The Bible says to think of things that are true and __good__
2. You may look at my cookbook as you __cook__ the food.
3. Tim took his jacket that has a __hood__
4. The class __stood__ to say the pledge to the flag.
5. The water felt cool as we put our foot in the __brook__

Remember! Other ways to spell the vowel digraph sound of o͝o are:
u as in pull, o as in wolf, and ou as in should.

◆Complete these sentences with words from the box at the right.

		should
		Could
1. We __should__ remember to __put__ our books in our desks.		push
2. God made the wild __wolf__ to be similar to a dog.		bush
3. __Could__ you please give me a __push__ on the swing?		wolf
4. Eric could not get the __bull__ to go in the barn.		full
5. The bull __would__ go in if his dog Butch barked at it.		bull
6. Sue sees a big __bush__ that is __full__ of red roses.		put
		would

Page 36

Purpose

To reinforce the sound of **ow** and **ou** as in the words *cow* and *house*.

Lesson

Listen as your student reads the words from **Chart 22** (found on page 186 in the workbook). This may take some time, but it will be very helpful.

Notice the spelling of the following words as you read them:

flower	vowel	clown
tower	towel	gown
shower	frown	crown
owl	town	cow

Listen as your student reads all of the words on the lists and gives the answers to the lesson orally before he completes it independently.

Page 37

Purpose

To review the sound of **ow** and **ou** as in the words *owl* and *count*.

Lesson

Review the previous lesson with the student. Does he think his printing is as neat as it should be?

Review the sound of **ow** and **ou**. Listen to him read the words on **Chart 22**. Repetition greatly helps to confirm any lesson. Use drills whenever it is necessary for strengthening reading skills. You may want to take turns; you read one word or column, and he reads the next word or column.

Listen as your student reads all of the words on the lists and gives the answers to the lesson orally before he completes it independently.

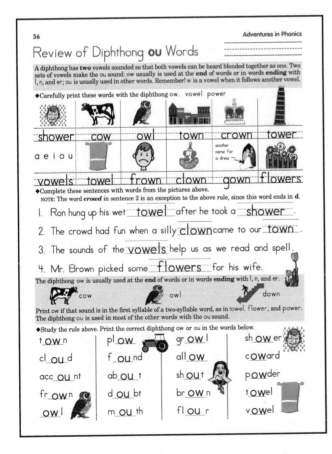

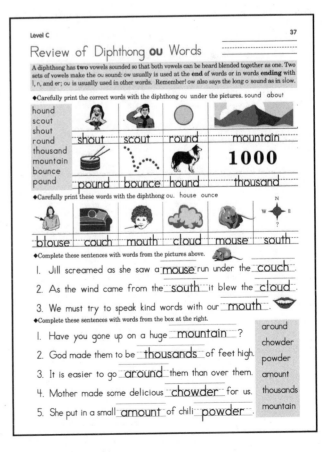

Page 38

Purpose

To reinforce the sound of **oi** and **oy** as in the words *coin* and *joy*.

Lesson

Listen as the words from **Chart 21** (found on page 186 in the workbook) are read.

Discuss that **oi** is usually followed by another consonant or two, but the **oy** usually is at the end of a word or syllable.

Notice the spelling of the following words as you read them.

toys	coin	boil
boy	point	poison

Listen as your student reads all of the words on the lists and gives the answers to the lesson orally before he completes it independently.

Note: The answer under the picture of the toys at the top of page 38 may be *toy* or *toys*. However, the second answer for sentence #2 below it requires the singular word *toy*.

Page 39

Purpose

To review the sound of **oi** and **oy** as in the words *broil* and *toy*.

Lesson

Have a quick review of the previous lesson with the student. Listen as your student reads the words from **Chart 21** again.

Review the fact that **oi** is usually followed by another consonant or two, but the **oy** usually is at the end of a word or syllable.

Notice the spelling of the following words as you read them:

oil	soil	noise
coil	foil	joints

Have the student give the answers to the lesson orally before he completes the page independently.

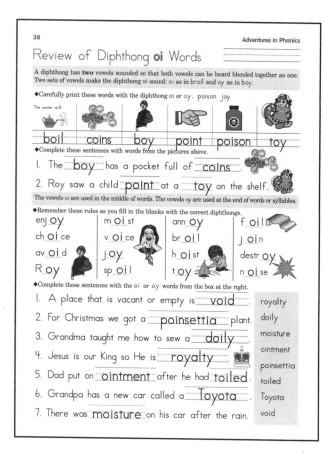

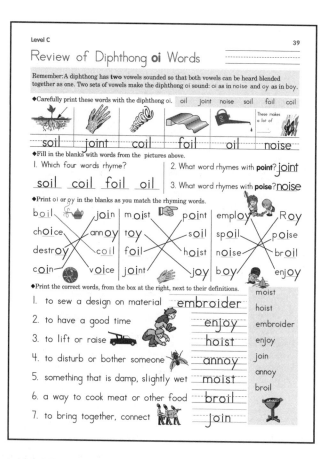

Page 40

Purpose

To review the sound of **är** as in the word <u>ark</u>.

Lesson

Listen to your student read the words from **Chart 24** (found on page 187 in the workbook).

Notice the spelling of the following words as you read them:

star	cart	arch
jar	arm	march
card	farm	yarn
harp	shark	barn

If you have written these words on the board, please erase them before the student does the lesson because they are used in this lesson.

Listen and help as your student gives the answers to the lesson orally before he completes it independently.

Page 41

Purpose

To reinforce the sound of **är** as in the word <u>ark</u>.

Lesson

Review the previous lesson with the student. Does he think his printing is as neat as it should be?

Notice the spelling of the following words as you read them:

ark	bar	dart
bark	car	garden

If you have written these words on the board, please erase them before the student does the lesson because they are used in this lesson.

Listen to him review the words from **Chart 24**.

Listen as the student gives the answers to the lesson orally before he completes it independently.

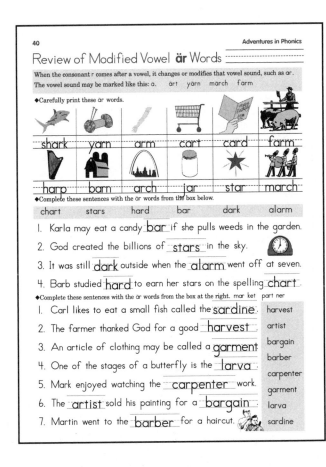

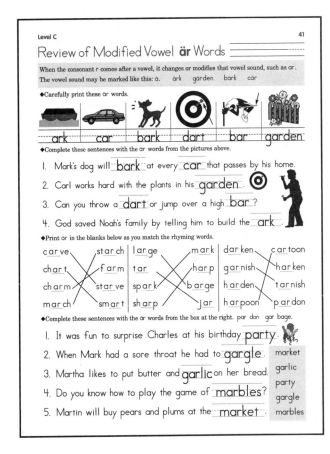

Page 42

Purpose

To review the sound of **ôr** as in the word *storm*.

Lesson

Listen as your student reads the words from **Chart 25** (found on page 187 in the workbook).

Notice the spelling of the following words as you read them:

corn	horse	fork
horn	shore	storm
acorn	store	fort
thorn	cord	north

If you have written these words on the board, please erase them before the student does the lesson because they are used in this lesson.

Help when necessary as the student gives the answers to the lesson orally before he completes it independently.

Page 43

Purpose

To reinforce the sound of **ôr** as in the word *chore*.

Lesson

Review the previous lesson with the student. Does he think his printing is as neat as it should be?

Have him review the words on **Chart 25**.

Notice the spelling of the following words as you read them:

store	shore	score
horse	core	sore

If you have written these words on the board, please erase them before the student does the lesson because they are used in this lesson.

Listen as he gives the answers to the lesson orally before he completes it independently.

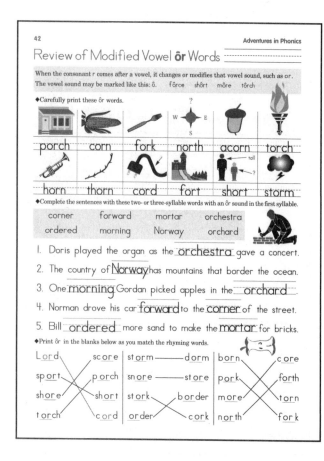

Page 44

Purpose
To teach the sound of **ûr** as in the words *verse*, *girl*, and *church*.

Lesson
Carefully review this sound with the three sets of letters **er**, **ir**, and **ur**. Listen as your student reads the words in the first five columns on **Chart 26** (found on page 187 in the workbook).

Notice the spelling of the following words as you read them:

fern	first	church
verse	third	turtle
sister	bird	nurse
brother	girl	purse

If you have written these words on the board, please erase them before the student does the lesson because they are used in this lesson.

Go over the directions, listen and help as your student gives the answers to the lesson orally before he completes it independently.

Page 45

Purpose
To teach the sound of **ûr** as in the words *person*, *bird*, and *turkey*.

Lesson
Review the previous lesson. Does the student think his printing is as neat as it should be?

Again review this sound with the three sets of letters **er**, **ir**, and **ur**. Listen to your student read the words in the first five columns on **Chart 26**.

Notice the spelling of the following words as you read them:

mother	shirt	curls
father	skirt	turkey

If you have written these words on the board, please erase them before the student does the lesson because they are used in this lesson.

Go over the directions and listen as he gives the answers to the lesson orally before he completes it independently.

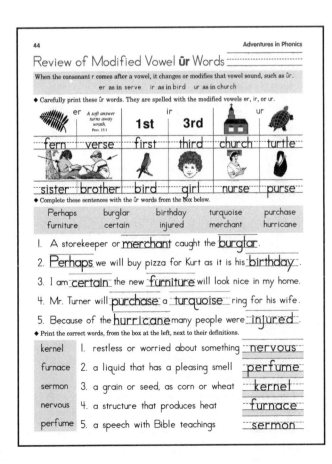

Page 46

Purpose

To review the sound of **ûr** as in the words *earth* and *(w)orld*.

Lesson

Spend as much time as needed for learning these words well.

Listen to your student read the words in the last two columns of **Chart 26** (found on page 187 in the workbook).

Notice the spelling of the following words as you read them:

world   work   worm

earth   words   pearl

Erase these words from the board before the student does the page because they are used in this lesson.

Listen as your student reads all of the words on the lists and gives the answers to the lesson orally before he completes it independently.

Note: The answer under the picture of a globe at the top of page 46 may be either *world* or *earth*.

Page 47

Purpose

To reinforce the sound of **ûr** as in the words *earth* and *(w)orld*.

Lesson

Review the previous lesson. Does your student think his printing is as neat as it should be?

Have him review the words in the last two columns on **Chart 26**.

Listen as he gives the answers to the lesson orally before he completes it independently.

As it is suggested for all of the lessons, correct his work the same day it is completed, talk about any errors, and have them corrected right away.

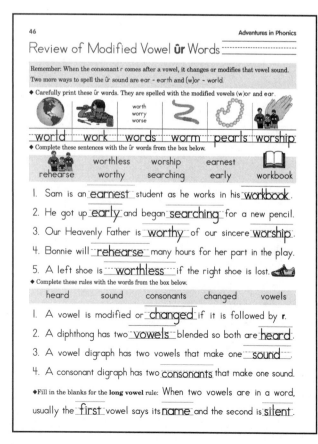

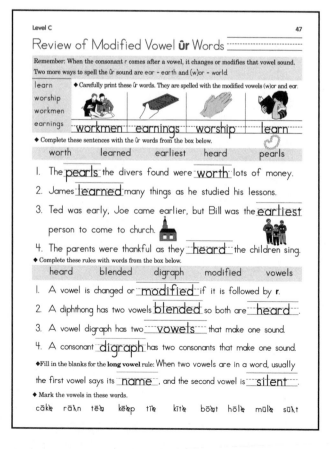

Page 48

Purpose

To review all the ways of spelling the sound of **âr** as in the word *square*.

Lesson

Carefully review with the student each of the sets of letters that can have the **âr** sound. Listen to him read the words from **Chart 27** (found on page 187 in the workbook).

Notice the spelling of the following words as you read them:

parrot	pear	chair
carrot	bear	stair
hare	cherry	pair
square	berry	hair

Erase these words from the board before the student does the page because they are used in this lesson.

Listen as your student reads and gives the answers to the lesson orally before he completes it independently.

Page 49

Purpose

To review the ways of spelling the sound of **âr** as in the word *share*, as well as the sound of **ûr** as in the word *church*.

Lesson

Talk with the student about the work done on the previous lesson. Does he think his printing is as neat as it should be?

Review each of the sets of letters that can have the **âr** sound. Listen as he again reads the words from **Chart 27**.

Notice the spelling of the following words as you read them:

Thursday	marry	share
turkey	carry	square
circus	pear	worm
circle	bear	world

Erase these words from the board before the student does the page because they are used in this lesson.

Have him give the answers to the lesson orally before he completes it independently.

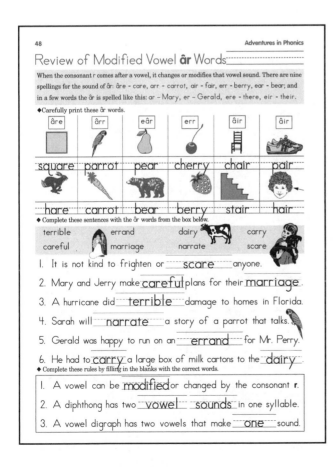

Page 50

Purpose

To review the sound of ô as in the words *frog, small, claw,* and *laundry*.

Lesson

Carefully review the four sets of letters that can have the ô sound: fr<u>o</u>g, sm<u>all</u>, cl<u>aw</u>, and l<u>au</u>ndry.

Take turns as you and your student read the words in the first five columns on **Chart 30** (found on page 188 in the workbook). This may take some time, but patience and encouragement will be most beneficial.

Notice the spelling of the following words as you read them:

c l o t h   d o g   s o n g

m o t h   f r o g   c r o s s

Erase these words from the board before the student does the page because they are used in this lesson.

Listen as your student reads and gives the answers to the lesson orally before he completes it independently.

Page 51

Purpose

To reinforce the sound of ô as in the words *daughter* and *thought*.

Lesson

Review the work done on the previous lesson.

Review the six sets of letters that can make the ô sound. **o**, **al**, **au**, **aw**, **augh**, and **ough**. Mention that the letters **gh** are silent in these words.

Have him read **Chart 30**, especially the last column.

Notice the spelling of the following words as you read them:

b a l l   c a l l   s t r a w

t a l k   w a l k   h a w k

f a l l   s a w   c r a w l

s t a l k   p a w   f a w n

Erase these words from the board before the student does the page because they are used in this lesson.

Have him give the answers to the lesson orally before he completes it independently.

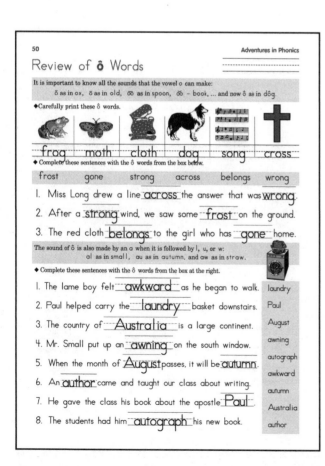

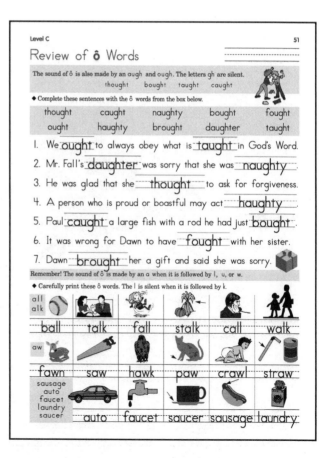

Page 52

Purpose

To review the words having sets of letters with a silent letter in each set such as **gn** (*gnaw*), **gu** (*guess*), **mb** (*limb*), **mn** (*hymn*), **bt** (*doubt*), and **bu** (*build*).

Lesson

Study the sets of sounds at the top of the lesson. Spend as much time as necessary to listen to your student work his way through the entire lesson orally. Encourage him to do his work carefully.

Tell him to think of the silent letters as he reads the following words:

lamb	guard	built
comb	guide	build
thumb	gnu	doubt
climb	gnaw	debt
guess	gnat	guitar
guest	buy	hymn

Carefully go over the entire lesson with the student, having him give the answers orally before completing the page independently.

Page 53

Purpose

To reinforce the words having sets of letters with a silent letter in each set such as **gn** (*gnaw*), **gu** (*guess*), **mb** (*limb*), **mn** (*hymn*), **bt** (*doubt*), and **bu** (*build*).

Lesson

Review these sets of sounds with silent letters: **gn**, **gu**, **mb**, **mn**, **bt**, and **bu**.

Have your student read the following words until he knows them well:

guess	gnash	thumb
guest	gnaw	buy
guard	lamb	doubt
guide	comb	sign

Use as much time as necessary to listen to your student work his way through the entire lesson orally. Encourage him to do his work carefully.

After he has given the answers orally, he should complete the page independently.

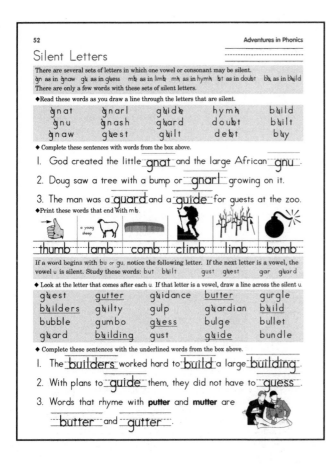

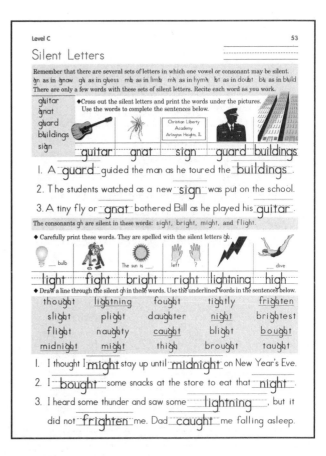

Page 54

Purpose

To review the sounds of the sets of letters with silent consonants such as **lf** (ha*lf*), **lk** (ta*l*k), **tch** (wa*t*ch), **lm** (pa*l*m), and **rh** (*rh*yme).

Lesson

Discuss the sets of sounds at the top of the lesson. Spend as much time as necessary to study these sets of letters.

As the student reads the following words, tell him to think of the silent letters, as in *walk*, *patch*, and *rhinoceros*:

walk	palm	pitch
talk	calm	pitcher
chalk	psalm	stitch
stalk	hatch	rhyme
calf	catch	rhubarb
half	match	rhythm

Have your student give the answers orally before completing the page independently. Encourage him to do his work carefully.

Page 55

Purpose

To reinforce the sounds of the sets of letters which have silent consonants such as **kn** (*k*now), **wr** (*w*rite), and **rh** (*rh*yme).

Lesson

Review the work done on the previous lesson. Does the student think his printing is as neat as it should be?

Carefully review with the student the sets of sounds at the top of the lesson before studying the page.

As he reviews the following words, tell him to think of the silent letters, as in *rhyme*, *know*, and *write*:

rhythm	knob	wreath
rhyme	knife	wrench
know	knit	write
knew	knuckles	wrist

Go over the entire lesson, having your student give the answers orally before completing the page.

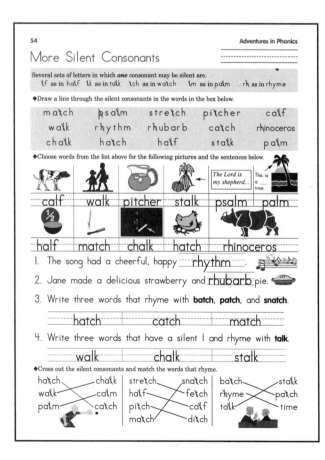

Page 56

Purpose

To review the sounds of the sets of letters with silent consonants such as **sc** as in *scent* and *muscles*, **st** as in *listen*, and **ft** as in *often*.

Lesson

Talk to your student about the work done on the previous lesson. Does he think his printing is as neat as it should be?

Discuss with him the sets of sounds at the top of the lesson. Review as much as necessary to learn the lesson. Notice the silent **t** and silent **c** in the words below:

fasten	thistle	scenery
listen	glisten	scissors
wrestle	scene	muscle

Have your student give the answers orally before completing the page independently. Encourage him to do his work carefully.

Page 57

Purpose

To reinforce the sounds of the sets of letters with silent consonants such as **sc** as in *scent* and *muscles*, **st** as in *listen*, and **ft** as in *often*.

To learn that **h** is silent in *honest*, *honor*, and *hour*.

Lesson

When **h** is silent, the short vowel **o** is heard. The indefinite article **an** is used with these words.

an honest boy, **an h**onor, **an h**our

Review with your student the sets of sounds at the top of this lesson. Then listen as the following words are read correctly without saying the silent letters:

often	scent	hymns
listen	whistle	doubt
science	scissors	thistle
fasten	wrinkle	scientist

Go over the entire lesson, having your student give the answers orally before completing the page.

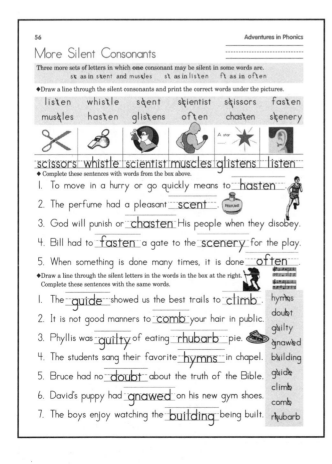

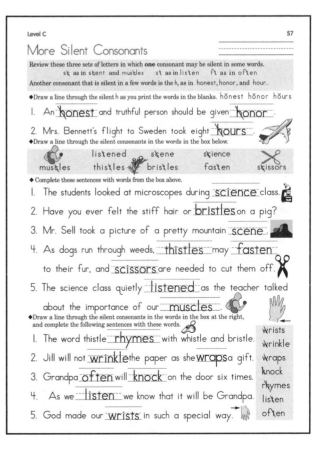

Page 58

Purpose

To review silent vowels and consonants.

Lesson

Write the following list of words on the board and listen to your student read them quickly. Review the vowels that are silent. Have him mark the vowels in the following words, as shown at the top of the lesson.

gāmé	trāɪn	prūné
smōké	fāɪnt	glōbé
stēɑm	trūé	stēͤr
brāɪn	whīté	drāɪn
whēɑt	tāmé	drēɑm

You may want him to look back on previous lessons to review the words with silent letters.

When you feel that he knows the words well, have your student complete the answers orally before completing the page independently.

Page 59

Purpose

To review silent vowels and consonants.

Lesson

Review the previous lesson. Write the following list of words on the board and listen to your student read them quickly. Review the vowels that are silent. Have him mark the vowels in the following words, as shown at the top of the lesson.

snāké	pāɪnt	glīdé
stōné	blūé	sāmé
grāɪn	whīlé	frāmé
whēͤl	nāmé	quāɪl

It may be helpful for him to look back on previous lessons to review the words with silent letters.

When you feel that your student knows the words well, have him complete the answers orally before completing the page independently.

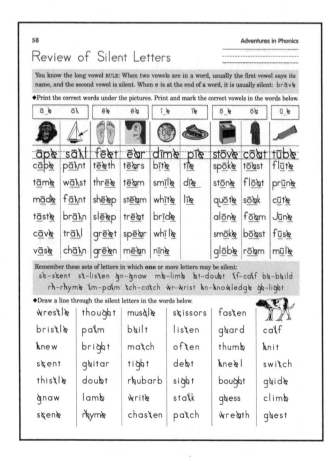

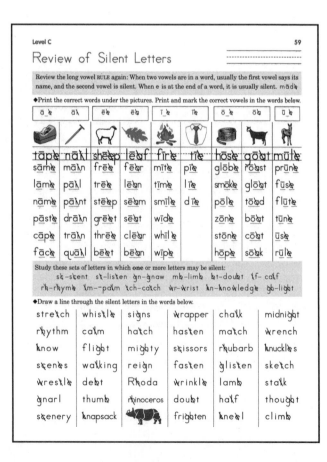

Page 60

Purpose

To review the seven sounds made by the digraph **ou**.

Lesson

Have the student read the following sets of words several times, listening to himself so as to hear the different sounds:

round   you   four

cloud   cougar   court

Have your student read these sets of words several times:

tough   boulder

country   shoulder

would   bought

could   thought

When you feel that he knows the words in the lesson well as he answers orally, encourage your student to carefully complete the work independently.

Page 61

Purpose

To review the seven sounds made by the digraph **ou**.

Lesson

Listen to the student read the following words and sounds, reading from left to right:

shout	found	mouse
you	coupon	soup
rough	country	touch
would	could	should
four	court	mourn
though	boulder	soul
bought	thought	cough

When you feel that your student knows the words in the lesson well as he answers orally, encourage him to carefully complete the work independently.

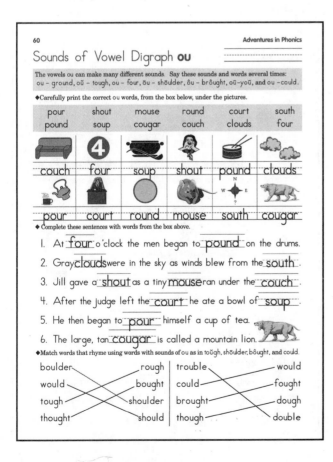

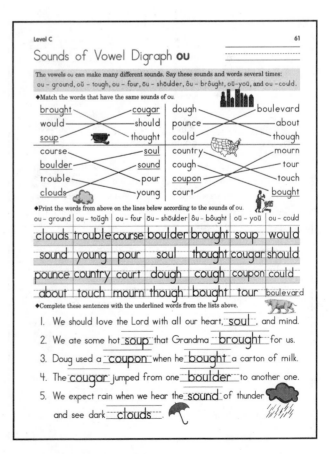

Page 62

Purpose

To review the four sounds made by **ear**.

Lesson

Quickly review the seven sounds made by **ou** in the previous lesson, perhaps reading the words in the center of the right column on page 31 of this manual. Have the student read the following sets of words with **ear** several times, listening to himself so as to hear the different sounds:

ear	earn	wear	heart
spear	learn	bear	
beard	heard	pear	
hear	pearl	tear	
dear	early		
near	earth		

Go through the lesson and have the student give the answers orally before completing the work independently.

Page 63

Purpose

To review the eight sets of letters which make the sound of **âr: ar, ear, are, air, err, arr, ere,** and **eir**.

Lesson

Quickly review the previous lesson on the four sounds made by **ear**. It would be good to read the lists across from this lesson of the teacher's manuel.

Discuss the meaning of the words **there** and **their**.

There is a picture of *their* house.

Have the student read the following sets of words which make the **âr** sound:

bear	pear	wear
share	hare	fare
hair	stairs	chair
berry	cherry	ferry
marry	carrot	parrot

Also review **Chart 27** on page 187 of the workbook.

Discuss the lesson and have the student give the answers orally before completing the work.

Note: In the second exercise on page 63 of the student workbook, the answer *berry* could also be *cherry*.

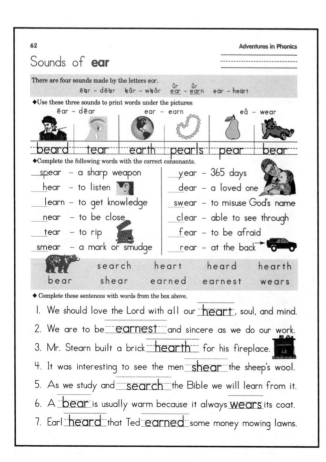

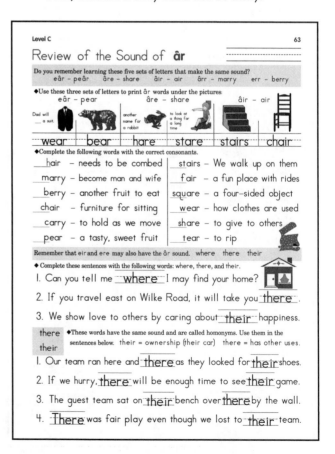

Page 64

Purpose
To review words with **y** and **w** as vowels.

Lesson
Carefully go over the information about **y** and **w** at the top of the page. Listen to your student read the words below that end with **y**:

play	try	softly	boy
pray	cry	baby	coy
stray	fly	happy	joy
delay	reply	berry	enjoy
away	apply	hurry	annoy

Have your student read the following words that use **w** as a vowel:

flew   crawl   throw   allow

threw   straw   below   brown

renew   thaw   yellow   crowd

Discuss the lesson and have him answer orally before he completes it independently.

Page 65

Purpose
To review words with **y** and **w** as vowels.

Lesson
Review the previous lesson with **y** and **w** as vowels.

The **y** is a silent vowel in digraphs **ay** and **ey**: s**ay**, k**ey**.

The **y** is a vowel in diphthong **oy**: ann**oy**, b**oy**.

The **y** has the long sound of **i**: sh**y**, repl**y**, appl**y**.

The **y** has the long sound of **e**: lad**y**, wind**y**, happ**y**.

The **w** is a vowel in digraphs **ow**, **ew**, and **aw**: sn**ow**, n**ew**, l**aw**.

The **w** is a vowel in diphthong **ow**: t**ow**n.

The **y** and **w** are consonants at the beginning of words or syllables: **y**es, **w**ind.

Discuss the lesson and have your student answer orally before he completes it independently.

Worksheet page 64

64   **Adventures in Phonics**

Letters **y** and **w** as Vowels

The letters y and w are consonants when they are at the beginning of words or syllables. yes wind
The y and w are vowels if they are part of digraphs or diphthongs. day boy snow jaw flew
☞y is a silent vowel in the digraph ay – day   ☞y is a vowel in the diphthong oy – boy
☞y has the sound of ī – try   ☞y has the sound of ē – lady
☞w is a silent vowel in the digraphs ow – snow, ew – new, and aw – law
☞w is a vowel in the diphthong ow – town

◆Print words ending with digraphs ay or ey. In the sentences, underline words with digraphs.

pray	key	spray	pay	turkey	donkey

1. <u>Ray</u> liked to <u>play</u> with the <u>gray donkey</u> with a <u>sway</u> back.
2. It will not <u>stray</u> or run <u>away</u>, but <u>may stay</u> near the <u>hay</u>.

◆Print words with vowel digraph aw, ew or ow. In the sentences, underline the words with digraphs.

screw	straw	blow	awning	snowman	pew

1. We <u>knew</u> the <u>fawn</u> had <u>grown</u> since we last <u>saw</u> it on our <u>lawn</u>.
2. I <u>know</u> the <u>snow</u> will soon <u>thaw</u> and <u>new</u> buds will <u>grow</u>.

◆Print words that end with the vowel y, which sounds like ī as in try.

fly	fry	cry	dry	shy	sky

bashful

◆Underline the words that end with the vowel y that sounds like ē as in tiny.
1. <u>Sally</u> was <u>happy</u> to see the <u>lady</u> with her <u>baby</u>.
2. The yellow <u>kitty swiftly</u> ran away from the <u>funny puppy</u>.
3. God makes <u>every</u> day to be <u>sunny</u>, <u>chilly</u>, <u>windy</u>, or calm.

Worksheet page 65

Level C   **65**

Letters **y** and **w** as Vowels

The letters y and w are consonants when they are at the beginning of words or syllables. yes wind
The y and w are vowels if they are part of digraphs or diphthongs. day boy crowd jaw flew

◆Print words with the diphthong ow. Underline words in the sentences with the diphthong ow.

crown	town	cow	frown	clown	shower

1. Did you learn <u>how</u> to say the sounds of the <u>vowels</u>?
2. The <u>brown owl</u> flew away as it heard the <u>growl</u> of the dog.
3. A <u>crowd</u> was <u>allowed</u> to go up in the new <u>tower downtown</u>.

◆Print words with diphthongs oi or oy. Underline words in the sentences with these diphthongs.

toys	poison	point	coin	boy	joint

1. <u>Boys</u> and girls should <u>avoid</u> making too much <u>noise</u>.
2. <u>Roy</u> and <u>Joyce</u> <u>enjoy</u> helping to <u>hoist</u> the flag each morning.
3. <u>Lloyd</u> and <u>Floyd</u> were <u>joyful</u> as their grandparents visited them.

◆Underline the y and w if they are vowels. sta**y** ke**y** sill**y** stra**w** clo**w**n blo**w**

window	wonderfully	yearly	monkey
lazy	pretty	yawn	jolly
yellow	joyful	wooly	flown
fellow	turkey	yummy	crawl
yesterday	youngster	windy	flower
tomorrow	yoyo	wavy	trolley
Wednesday	willow	loyal	town

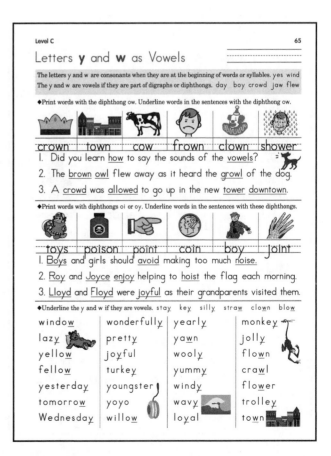

Page 66

Purpose

To review words that are spelled with **ei** and **ey** that have the long sound of **a** as in *eight*.

Lesson

Have your student read the words below as he notices their spellings with **ei** and **ey**:

e i g h t	r e i g n s	t h e y
e i g h t h	w e i g h t	w h e y
e i g h t y	v e i n s	p r e y
n e i g h	r e i n s	o b e y
s l e i g h	f r e i g h t	s u r v e y

Discuss the lesson and have your student answer orally before he completes it independently.

Page 67

Purpose

To review words that are spelled with **ei** and **ey** that have the long sound of **a** as in *eight*.

Lesson

Review the previous lesson, perhaps by having the student read the completed sentences.

There are no special rules as to when to use **ei** or **ey**; the spelling of the words must be learned by study.

Listen as he reviews the following words:

e i g h t	w e i g h t	h e y
e i g h t h	v e i l	t h e y
e i g h t y	v e i n s	w h e y
n e i g h	r e i n s	p r e y
s l e i g h	r e i g n s	o b e y
w e i g h	f r e i g h t	s u r v e y

Discuss the lesson and have your student answer orally before he completes it independently.

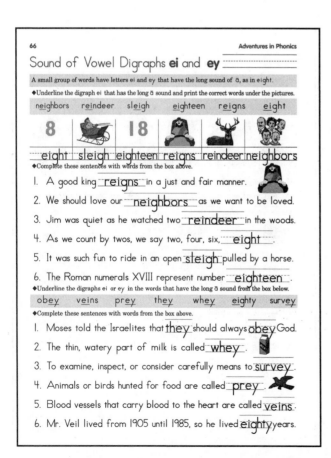

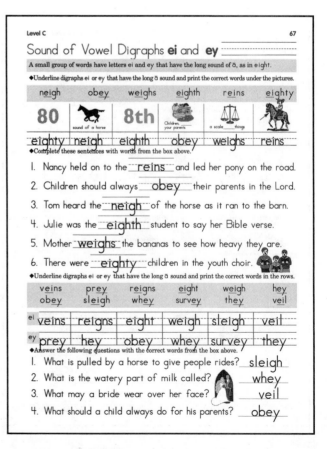

Page 68

Purpose

To review words that are spelled with **ie** that have the long sound of **e** as in *chief*.

Lesson

Study the directions at the top of the page. Listen to your student read the following words spelled with **ie**:

believe	chief	diesel
achieve	thief	field
relieve	grief	shield
pierce	belief	piece
fierce	relief	shriek

Say the poem at the bottom of the page several times. Mention that there are several words that do not follow this rule: either, leisure, neither, and seize.

Discuss the lesson and have your student answer orally before he completes it independently.

Page 69

Purpose

To review words that are spelled with **ie** that have the long sound of **e** as in *thief*.

Lesson

Review the previous lesson by reading the sentences in the middle of the page. Help your student read the following list of words, asking him to say the long vowel sound of **a**, **e**, or **i** for the sound that **ie** and **ei** make:

bel**ie**ve	f**ie**rce	rel**ie**f
t**ie**	r**ei**gns	d**ie**sel
ach**ie**ve	ch**ie**f	f**ie**ld
eight	sl**ei**gh	sh**ie**ld
v**ei**n	l**ie**	w**ei**gh
rel**ie**ve	gr**ie**f	p**ie**ce
p**ie**rce	v**ei**l	shr**ie**k

Discuss the lesson and have your student answer orally before he completes it independently.

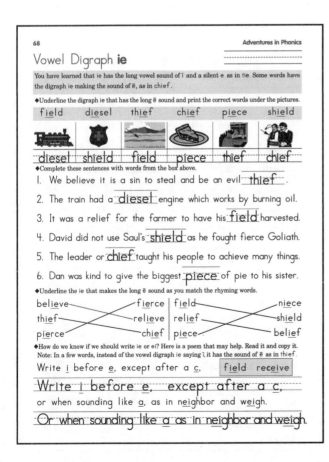

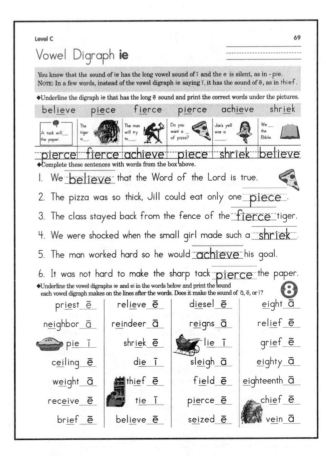

Page 70

Purpose

To review words spelled with the consonant digraphs **ch** (having the sounds of **ch**, **sh**, or **k**) and **th** (having the sounds of <u>th</u> as in *the* or **th** as in *thin*).

Lesson

Most **ch** words have the sound as in **church**, but it is important to know the other words as well. Listen to your student read each of the lists below, noticing the various sounds the digraphs **ch** and **th** make:

church	chef	Christ
chapter	chute	choir
chief	chiffon	chord
choice	chic	chorus
choose	machine	chemist

that	these	bath	thing
them	those	thank	think

Discuss the lesson and have your student answer orally before he completes it independently.

Page 71

Purpose

To review words that have **gh** and **ph** which make the sound of **f**.

To learn how a dictionary may show the way to sound out and pronounce words.

Lesson

Review the previous lesson. Listen to your student read the words below:

laugh	digraph	phonics
rough	phony	alphabet
dolphin	nephew	photo
graph	enough	hyphen
cough	phrase	trophy

Discuss the lesson and have your student answer orally before he completes it independently.

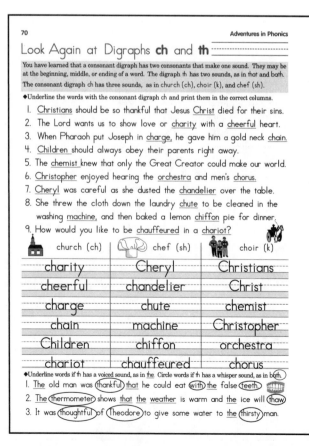

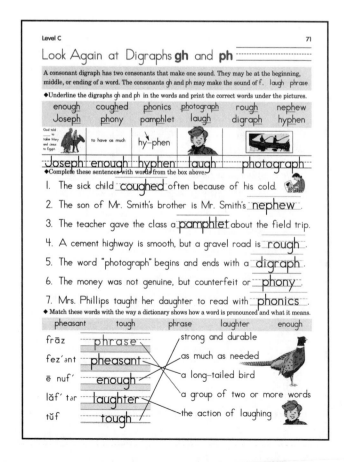

Page 72

Purpose

To review words that are spelled with consonant digraphs **th**, **ch**, **sh**, and **wh**, as well as **gh** and **ph**.

Lesson

Listen to your student read the words below:

church	phrase	rough
chef	children	alphabet
Christ	chiffon	lunch
shovel	chorus	chute
wheat	sheep	chemist
thumb	whisper	shadow
mother	thistle	whistle
laugh	brother	bath

Discuss the lesson and have your student answer orally before he completes it independently.

Note: In the last exercise on page 72 of the student workbook, the answer *where* could also be *there*.

Page 73

Purpose

To review the use of the indefinite articles **a** and **an**.

To review the three sounds of vowel digraph **ea**.

Lesson

Review the previous lesson by reading the sentences in the middle of the page.

Discuss the rules of this lesson:

1. The word **a** is used before words beginning with a *consonant*.

   a pumpkin, **a w**all, **a p**icture, **a d**oor

2. The word **an** is used before words beginning with a *vowel* or a vowel sound.

   an eagle, **an e**ye, **an u**mbrella, **an i**nch, **an h**our

Review the three sounds of vowel digraph **ea**:

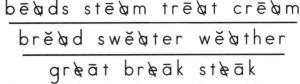

bēads stēam trēat crēam

brĕad swĕater wĕather

grēat brēak stēak

Discuss the lesson and have your student answer orally before he completes it independently.

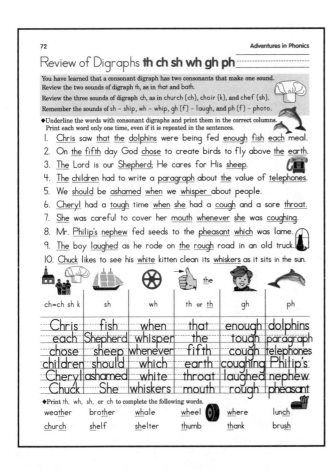

72   Adventures in Phonics

Review of Digraphs **th ch sh wh gh ph**

You have learned that a consonant digraph has two consonants that make one sound.
Review the two sounds of digraph th, as in that and bath.
Review the three sounds of digraph ch, as in church (ch), choir (k), and chef (sh).
Remember the sounds of sh – ship, wh – whip, gh (f) – laugh, and ph (f) – photo.

◆Underline the words with consonant digraphs and print them in the correct columns.
Print each word only one time, even if it is repeated in the sentences.

1. <u>Chris</u> saw <u>that</u> <u>the</u> dolphins were being fed <u>enough</u> <u>fish</u> <u>each</u> meal.
2. On <u>the</u> <u>fifth</u> day God <u>chose</u> to create birds to fly above <u>the</u> <u>earth</u>.
3. <u>The</u> Lord is our <u>Shepherd</u>; He cares for His <u>sheep</u>.
4. <u>The</u> <u>children</u> had to write a <u>paragraph</u> about <u>the</u> value of <u>telephones</u>.
5. We <u>should</u> be <u>ashamed</u> when we <u>whisper</u> about people.
6. <u>Cheryl</u> had a <u>tough</u> time <u>when</u> <u>she</u> had a <u>cough</u> and a sore <u>throat</u>.
7. <u>She</u> was careful to cover her <u>mouth</u> <u>whenever</u> <u>she</u> was <u>coughing</u>.
8. Mr. <u>Philip's</u> <u>nephew</u> fed seeds to the <u>pheasant</u> <u>which</u> was lame.
9. <u>The</u> boy <u>laughed</u> as he rode on <u>the</u> <u>rough</u> road in an old truck.
10. <u>Chuck</u> likes to see his <u>white</u> kitten clean its <u>whiskers</u> as it sits in the sun.

ch=ch sh k	sh	wh	th or th	gh	ph
Chris	fish	when	that	enough	dolphins
each	Shepherd	whisper	the	tough	paragraph
chose	sheep	whenever	fifth	cough	telephones
children	should	which	earth	coughing	Philip's
Cheryl	ashamed	white	throat	laughed	nephew
Chuck	She	whiskers	mouth	rough	pheasant

◆Print th, wh, sh, or ch to complete the following words.

weather	brother	whale	wheel	where	lunch
church	shelf	shelter	thumb	thank	brush

Level C   73

Using **a** and **an**

When one object is mentioned, the words a or an may be used when talking about that object.
1. The word a is used before a word that begins with a consonant. a dinosaur   a walrus
2. The word an is used before a word that begins with a vowel or vowel sound. an egg   an honor

◆Notice the beginning letter of each word and think of the RULES above, then print a or an.

a	giraffe	an	otter	an	anteater
an	eagle	a	hawk	an	opossum
an	eel	a	lemming	a	platypus
a	falcon	a	tiger	a	camel
a	peacock	a	squirrel	an	ibis
a	beagle	an	octopus	a	whale
a	gorilla	an	insect	a	shark

a	body
an	eye
a	brain
an	ear
a	soul

" You are worthy, our LORD, to receive glory and honor and power; for
You created all things, and by Your will they exist and were created." Rev. 4:11 NKJV

◆Think as you print a or an in the blanks to complete the sentences. Use capital letters when needed.

1. A good person cares about the needs of an animal.
2. God hates a lying tongue and a false witness.
3. An angry person makes trouble, but a gentle answer is good.
4. A wise son gives joy, but a foolish son brings grief.
5. A lazy person wants and gets nothing; a good worker is blessed.
6. A wise son listens to his father, but a mocker does not listen.

◆Think about the three sounds of ea. Print the words in the correct columns.

bread	steam	ēā	ĕă	ĕā
break	thread	treat	bread	break
treat	great	steam	thread	great

Page 74

Purpose

To become more familiar with words ending with **sure** and **zure**.

To review the use of **a** and **an**.

Lesson

Review the previous lesson, checking to see if the student understands when to use the articles **a** and **an**. Listen to your student read the words below which have the **zh** sound:

measure   pleasure   seizure

treasure   leisure   closure

Discuss the lesson and have your student answer orally before he completes it independently.

Page 75

Purpose

To become more familiar with words ending with **ture**.

Lesson

Review the previous lesson, checking for neatness, ability to quickly read the list of **zh** words, and knowing when to use articles **a** and **an**. Listen as the following words ending with **ture** (*cher*) are quickly read:

nature	puncture
mature	picture
lecture	creature
pasture	fracture
capture	denture
future	adventure

Discuss the lesson and have your student answer orally before he completes it independently.

---

74   Adventures in Phonics

The Syllables **sure** and **zure**

As you read these words ending with sure or zure, you can hear the letter s or z make the zh sound.
Listen as you say the following words: treasure, measure, pleasure, and seizure.

◆Print the words from the box at the left on the lines next to their definitions. Use them in the sentences below.

Mr. Jones treasured the pleasure of his leisure time relaxing under the azure sky.

seizure	a pleasant feeling	pleasure
pleasure	to find the size of an object	measure
leisure	object of great value	treasure
measure	a time to relax	leisure
treasure	color of a clear blue sky	azure
azure	the act of taking quickly	seizure

1. Sue used a ruler to __measure__ the size of the table.

2. Our family enjoys the __pleasure__ of being together.

3. Ken wanted his ceiling painted the color of __azure__.

4. Grandpa spent his __leisure__ time making wooden toys.

5. Mr. Tate was shocked at the tornado's __seizure__ of his barn.

6. We found a wonderful __treasure__ in Grandma's attic.

◆Remember these rules as you print a or an before these words.

1. The word a is used before a word that begins with a consonant: a walrus
2. The word an is used before a word that begins with a vowel or vowel sound: an apple an hour

a seal	a horse	a tiger	an ant
an elephant	an insect	a fish	a buffalo
an ostrich	an honor	a deer	an eagle

Level C   75

The Syllable **ture**

In these words, the syllable ture makes the cher sound.
Listen as you say the following words: pasture, mature, adventure, and nature.

◆Underline the letters ture in the following words and print them by their meanings below.

puncture	creature	lecture	pasture	fracture
picture	future	mature	nature	capture

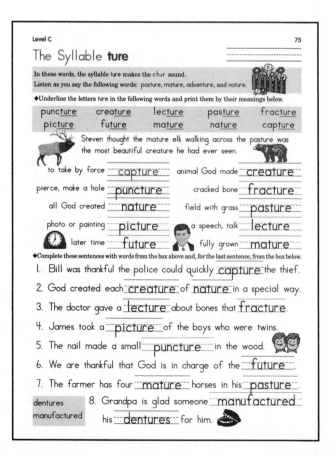

Steven thought the mature elk walking across the pasture was the most beautiful creature he had ever seen.

to take by force	capture	animal God made	creature
pierce, make a hole	puncture	cracked bone	fracture
all God created	nature	field with grass	pasture
photo or painting	picture	a speech, talk	lecture
later time	future	fully grown	mature

◆Complete these sentences with words from the box above and, for the last sentence, from the box below.

1. Bill was thankful the police could quickly __capture__ the thief.

2. God created each __creature__ of __nature__ in a special way.

3. The doctor gave a __lecture__ about bones that __fracture__.

4. James took a __picture__ of the boys who were twins.

5. The nail made a small __puncture__ in the wood.

6. We are thankful that God is in charge of the __future__.

7. The farmer has four __mature__ horses in his __pasture__.

| dentures | 8. Grandpa is glad someone __manufactured__ |
| manufactured | his __dentures__ for him. |

Page 76

Purpose
To review suffixes and syllables ending with **er**, **or**, and **ar**.

Lesson
Review the previous lessons, reading lists of the main words and some of the sentences. Explain that **er**, **or**, and **ar** may be added to words as suffixes (*worker, brighter*) or may always be a part of a word (*collar, power*). Listen to your student read the following words in which **er**, **or**, and **ar** are syllables—not suffixes:

shelter	calendar	beaver
father	burglar	doctor
mother	winter	collar
other	anchor	proper
power	color	bother
flavor	fever	sister

Discuss the lesson and have your student answer orally before he completes it independently.

Page 77

Purpose
To review when to add **s** or **es** to make words plural.

Lesson
Discuss with your student the rules about adding **s** or **es** to make words plural.

1. Usually an **s** is added to a *root* word to make it plural. Listen as the lists of words at the top of the lesson are read.

2. When words end with **s, x, z, sh,** or **ch, es** is usually added. The **e** makes the short vowel sound, causing the **es** to become a syllable, as in *dress ⇨ dresses, crash ⇨ crashes*. Listen as the lists of words in the middle of the lesson are read.

Discuss the lesson and have your student answer orally before he completes it independently.

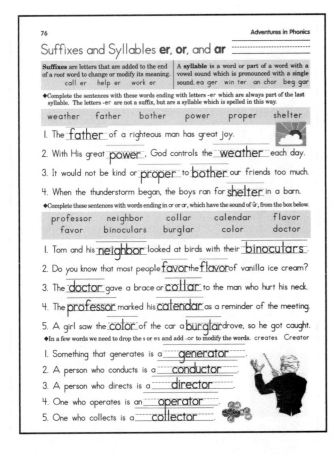

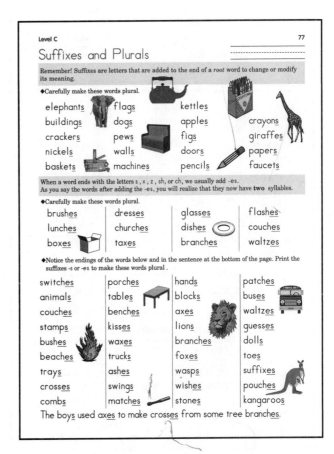

Page 78

Purpose

To review the three sounds the suffix **-ed** makes as a suffix.

To review adding the suffix **-ing** to words.

Lesson

Listen to your student read the words below, noticing that the **ed** makes three different sounds: **d**, **t**, and **əd**.

Discuss that in the last column of words, the **e** has a vowel sound which makes the **ed** to be a syllable.

feared	talked	rested
burned	chirped	handed
hauled	picked	mended
trained	pushed	printed
farmed	worked	guarded
called	jumped	listed

Discuss the lesson and have your student answer orally before he completes it independently.

Page 79

Purpose

To reinforce the following rules:

1. When a one-syllable, short vowel word ends with one consonant, double that consonant before adding a suffix beginning with a vowel: *win ⇨ winner*.

2. If the word ends with two consonants, just add the suffix: *test ⇨ testing*.

To review **y** as a vowel if added to the end of a word.

Lesson

Discuss the rules mentioned in the purpose section above. Listen as the following words are read, *noticing if a consonant is doubled before a suffix (beginning with a vowel) is added,* or if a suffix is just added.

skip	jump	paint
skipped	jumped	painter
clap	big	sun
clapping	biggest	sunny

Discuss the lesson and have your student answer orally before he completes it independently.

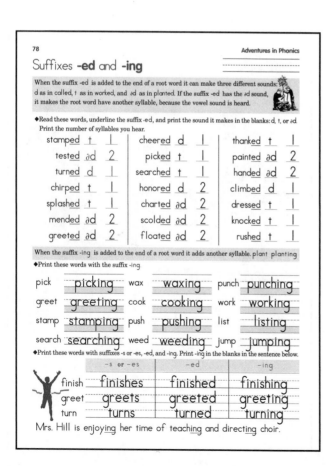

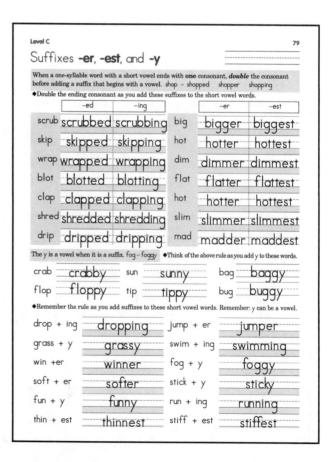

Page 80

Purpose
To reinforce the following rule:

When adding a suffix beginning with a conso-nant to a word, the suffix is added without changing the root word: *sin* ⇨ *sinful, rest* ⇨ *rest-less.*

Lesson
Discuss the rule in the purpose section above. Lis-ten to your student read the words below, noticing that the root words are not changed when adding suffixes beginning with consonants:

truth	care	fear
truthful	careless	fearless
use	thank	hope
useless	thankful	hopeful
pain	faith	sick
painful	faithful	sickness

Discuss the lesson and have your student answer orally before he completes it independently.

Page 81

Purpose
To reinforce the following rule:

When adding a suffix beginning with a conso-nant to a word, the suffix is added without changing the root word: *shy* ⇨ *shyly, sad* ⇨ *sad-ness.*

Lesson
Review the previous lesson and discuss the rule in the purpose section above. Listen as the words below are read, noticing that the root words are not changed when adding suffixes beginning with consonants:

soft	glad	still
softness	gladly	stillness
sweet	cold	kind
sweetly	coldness	kindly
sad	loud	ill
sadness	loudly	illness

Discuss the lesson and have your student answer orally before he completes it independently.

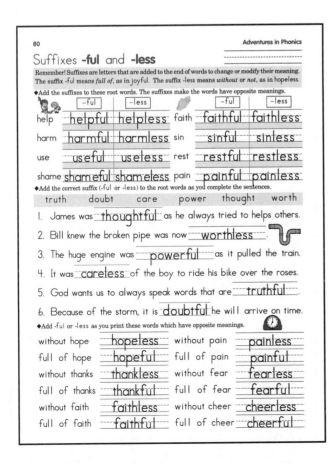

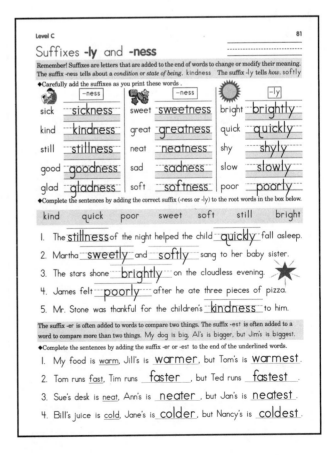

Page 82

Purpose

To review the following rule:

Drop the silent **e** when adding a suffix beginning with a vowel.

Lesson

Discuss the rule above. Some suffixes beginning with vowels are: **-ed, -er, -est, -ing, -y, -age, -ance,** and **-able**. After listening to your student read the words below, have him explain the rule.

take	store	smile
taking	storage	smiling
brave	like	trade
bravest	likable	traded
glide	large	close
glider	largest	closer

Discuss the lesson and have your student answer orally before he completes it independently.

Page 83

Purpose

To review four rules about adding suffixes beginning with a vowel.

To review adding suffixes beginning with a consonant.

Lesson

Discuss each of the rules that are printed at the top of the lesson. Have your student read and explain the rules about adding the suffixes to the following root words.

$$clip + ing = clipping$$
$$bake + ed = baked$$
$$jump + er = jumper$$
$$cream + y = creamy$$
$$insure + ance = insurance$$

Discuss the lesson and have your student answer orally before he completes it independently.

Note: Root words with more that one syllable are used in this lesson, such as *avail* (a•vail + a•ble = a•vail•a•ble); but the rules still apply, depending on the *last syllable* in each root word.

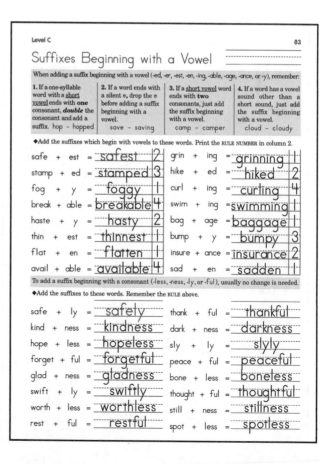

Page 84

Purpose
To review some of the rules about adding suffixes to words ending with **y**.

Lesson
Discuss each of the rules that are printed at the top of the lesson. Have your student read and explain the rules about adding the suffixes to the root words in the list below:

country + es = countries

turkey + s = turkeys

beauty + ful = beautiful

study + ing = studying

marry + age = marriage

plenty + ful = plentiful

Discuss the lesson and have your student answer orally before he completes it independently.

Page 85

Purpose
To review the rules about adding suffixes to words ending with **y**.

Lesson
Carefully discuss each of the rules that are printed at the top of the lesson. Have your student read and explain the rules about adding the suffixes to the following root words:

penny + less = penniless

monkey + s = monkeys

play + ful = playful

worry + ing = worrying

shy + ly = shyly

day + ly = daily

Discuss the lesson and have your student answer orally before he completes it independently.

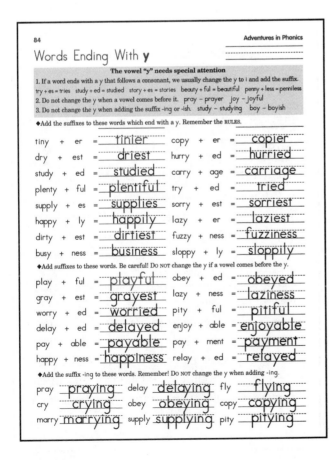

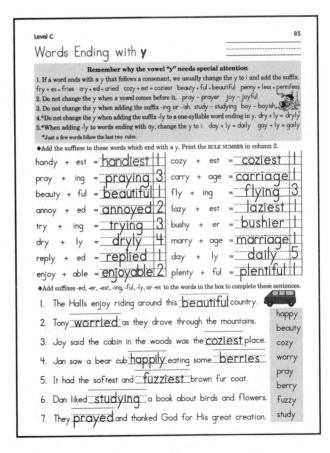

Page 86

Purpose
To learn how to easily read words ending with -**tion**.

Lesson
Spend a short time reviewing the previous lessons about suffixes. Listen as your student reads the list of words below which end with -**tion** (*shun*):

action	invention	lotion
faction	mention	motion
traction	affection	notion
nation	section	addition
station	fiction	subtraction
vacation	friction	fraction

Discuss the lesson and have your student answer orally before he completes it independently.

Page 87

Purpose
To learn how to easily read words ending with -**tion**.

Lesson
Review the previous lesson. Explain and discuss the rule about adding -**ion** to words ending in **e**.

pollute + ion = pollution
educate + ion = education
donate + ion = donation
institute + ion = institution
operate + ion = operation

Discuss the lesson and have your student answer orally before he completes it independently.

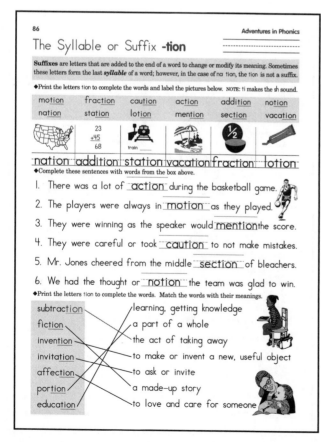

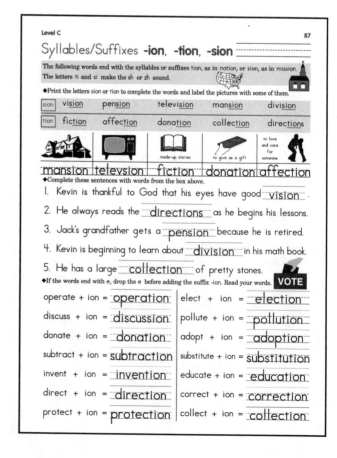

Page 88

Purpose
To review words with suffixes -en, -ity, -ive, and -some.

Lesson
Review the lesson on page 83 in the workbook about adding suffixes beginning with a vowel. Listen as your student reads and explains the rules to the words in the list below:

$$\text{relate} + \text{ive} = \text{relative}$$
$$\text{act} + \text{ive} = \text{active}$$
$$\text{ripe} + \text{en} = \text{ripen}$$
$$\text{forbid} + \text{en} = \text{forbidden}$$
$$\text{humid} + \text{ity} = \text{humidity}$$
$$\text{lone} + \text{some} = \text{lonesome}$$

Discuss the lesson and have your student answer orally before he completes it independently.

Page 89

Purpose
To review words that end with suffixes which begin with a vowel.

Lesson
Carefully study the rules at the top of the lesson. Listen as your student reads and explains how to add the suffixes.

Give help whenever needed.

Discuss the lesson and have your student answer orally before he completes it independently.

Note: Root words with more that one syllable are used in this lesson, such as **forget** (for•get + a•ble = for•get•ta•ble); but the rules still apply, depending on the **last syllable** in each root word.

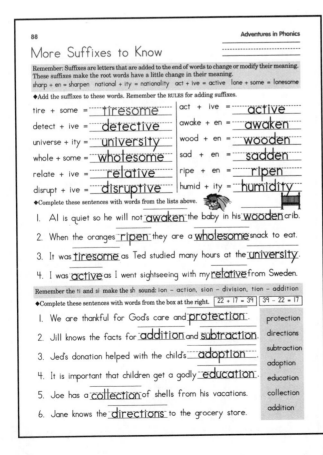

---

88   Adventures in Phonics

More Suffixes to Know

Remember: Suffixes are letters that are added to the end of words to change or modify their meaning. These suffixes make the root words have a little change in their meaning.

sharp + en = sharpen   national + ity = nationality   act + ive = active   lone + some = lonesome

◆Add the suffixes to these words. Remember the RULES for adding suffixes.

tire + some =	**tiresome**	act + ive =	**active**
detect + ive =	**detective**	awake + en =	**awaken**
universe + ity =	**university**	wood + en =	**wooden**
whole + some =	**wholesome**	sad + en =	**sadden**
relate + ive =	**relative**	ripe + en =	**ripen**
disrupt + ive =	**disruptive**	humid + ity =	**humidity**

◆Complete these sentences with words from the lists above.

1. Al is quiet so he will not **awaken** the baby in his **wooden** crib.

2. When the oranges **ripen** they are a **wholesome** snack to eat.

3. It was **tiresome** as Ted studied many hours at the **university**.

4. I was **active** as I went sightseeing with my **relative** from Sweden.

Remember the ti and si make the sh sound: ion – action, sion – division, tion – addition

◆Complete these sentences with words from the box at the right.   22 + 17 = 39   39 – 22 = 17

1. We are thankful for God's care and **protection**.

2. Jill knows the facts for **addition** and **subtraction**.

3. Jed's donation helped with the child's **adoption**.

4. It is important that children get a godly **education**.

5. Joe has a **collection** of shells from his vacations.

6. Jane knows the **directions** to the grocery store.

protection
directions
subtraction
adoption
education
collection
addition

Level C   **89**

Review of Words with Suffixes

Remember these rules when adding a suffix beginning with a vowel.

-ed -er -est -en -ing -able -age -ance -ity -ive -ion -y

| **1.** If a one-syllable word with a short vowel ends with one consonant, **double** the consonant and add a suffix. hop – hopped | **2.** If a word ends with a silent e, drop the e before adding a suffix beginning with a vowel. save – saving | **3.** If a short vowel word ends with two consonants, just add the suffix beginning with a vowel. camp – camper | **4.** If a word has a vowel sound other than a short sound, just add the suffix beginning with a vowel. cloud – cloudy |

◆Add the suffixes which begin with vowels to these words. Print the RULE NUMBER in column 2.

tackle + ed =	**tackled**	2	haste + y =	**hasty**	2
bake + ing =	**baking**	2	bag + age =	**baggage**	1
insure + ance =	**insurance**	2	saddle + ing =	**saddling**	2
dark + est =	**darkest**	4	disrupt + ive =	**disruptive**	3
divide + ing =	**dividing**	2	national + ity =	**nationality**	4
defense + ive =	**defensive**	2	wet + est =	**wettest**	1
plot + ed =	**plotted**	1	forget + able =	**forgettable**	1
avail + able =	**available**	4	plan + er =	**planner**	1
train + er =	**trainer**	4	adopt + ion =	**adoption**	3

◆Print the root word in one column and the suffix in the other. Remember that you may have to add a silent e to the root word, change the i to a y, or take off a consonant in a short vowel word.

busily	**busy**	**ly**	supplies	**supply**	**es**
biggest	**big**	**est**	baggage	**bag**	**age**
enjoyable	**enjoy**	**able**	lazier	**lazy**	**er**
boneless	**bone**	**less**	assurance	**assure**	**ance**
careful	**care**	**ful**	business	**busy**	**ness**
copier	**copy**	**er**	nationality	**national**	**ity**
weakest	**weak**	**est**	acceptable	**accept**	**able**

Page 90

Purpose

To review adding suffixes to words ending with **y**.

Lesson

Briefly review the rules for adding suffixes that were covered in the previous lesson.

In this lesson, the five rules about adding suffixes to words ending with y (*introduced on pages 84 and 85 of the workbook*) are reinforced. Carefully go over these rules at the top of the lesson, using the words from the list below. Ask the student which rule applies.

country+es = countries

heavy+ness = heaviness

fry+ing = frying

sly+ly = slyly

day+ly = daily

play+ed = played

Carefully and thoroughly discuss the lesson and have your student answer orally before he completes it independently.

Page 91

Purpose

To review words ending with suffixes.

Lesson

Review the rules at the top of the last two lessons.

Carefully discuss the lesson and have the student answer orally before he completes it independently.

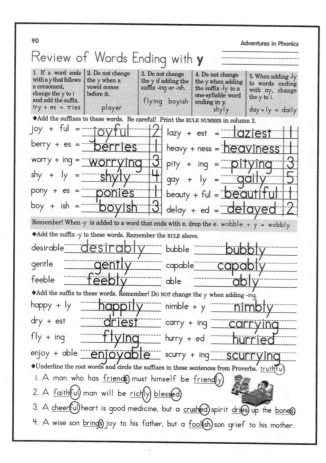

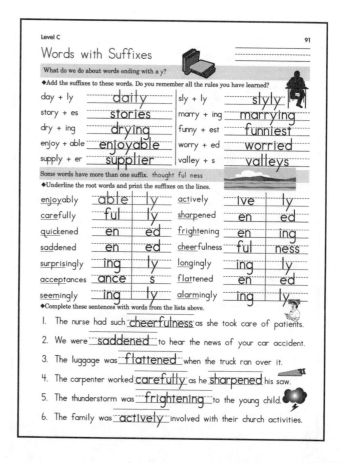

Page 92

Purpose
To review dividing words ending with suffixes.

Lesson
Your student should not have difficulty with this lesson. Discuss the rule about never dividing a one-syllable word. Each syllable must have a vowel sound.

Listen to him give the answers to the lesson orally before he completes it independently.

Page 93

Purpose
To review how to change words ending with **y** into plural words.

Lesson
Your student should know these two rules well, since he has studied them in the previous lessons.

Carefully and thoroughly discuss the lesson and have him answer orally before he completes it independently.

---

92   Adventures in Phonics

Review of Suffixes

Suffixes are letters that are added to the end of words to change or modify their meaning.
A suffix is a syllable in itself if it has a vowel sound. test-ed   harm-less   soft-ly
Always remember that a one-syllable word is never divided. walked

◆Divide these words into syllables when the suffix has a vowel sound in it.

kindness	kind-ness	called	called	talked	talked
worked	worked	laughing	laugh-ing	quicker	quick-er
gladly	glad-ly	softest	soft-est	shyly	shy-ly
tested	test-ed	melted	melt-ed	helped	helped
sicker	sick-er	loudest	loud-est	slowing	slow-ing
greatest	great-est	nicely	nice-ly	poorly	poor-ly

Remember! If a word ends with s, x, z, ch or sh, add -es to make it plural. box-es (two syllables)

◆Print these words as plural words, dividing them into syllables.

lunch	lunch-es	bush	bush-es	fox	fox-es
dress	dress-es	buzz	buzz-es	bench	bench-es
dish	dish-es	kiss	kiss-es	glass	glass-es
church	church-es	tax	tax-es	ax	ax-es

◆As we think about compound words again, divide the following words into syllables.
Caution! There are some one-syllable words among the lists. What do you do about dividing them?

necktie	neck-tie	redbird	red-bird	footprint	foot-print
airway	air-way	seagull	sea-gull	headache	head-ache
peanut	pea-nut	thought	thought	streams	streams
treetop	tree-top	highway	high-way	oatmeal	oat-meal
strength	strength	mailbox	mail-box	seaweed	sea-weed
sideways	side-ways	outside	out-side	hotdog	hot-dog
doorknob	door-knob	strain	strain	branch	branch

Level C   93

Plural Words Ending with **y**

1. If a word ends with a y that follows a consonant, change the y to i and add the suffix.	2. Do **not** change the y when a vowel comes before it.
try + es = tries	plays boys monkeys

◆Make these words plural. Print the number of the RULE that is used.

tray	trays 2	candy	candies 1	key	keys 2
puppy	puppies 1	copy	copies 1	story	stories 1
turkey	turkeys 2	donkey	donkeys 2	baby	babies 1
county	counties 1	pony	ponies 1	boy	boys 2
study	studies 1	berry	berries 1	cry	cries 1
toy	toys 2	daisy	daisies 1	city	cities 1
duty	duties 1	valley	valleys 2	fly	flies 1

◆Complete these sentences with plurals of the following words. Fill in the blanks at the bottom of the page.

chimney	beauty	melody	worry	hobby
raspberry	birthday	country	activity	medley

1. Jerry ate more raspberries than he brought home to his mother.
2. How old would you be if you have had 25 birthdays ?
3. The two groups or medleys of songs that Kay played for her piano recital had beautiful melodies
4. The bricklayer built two chimneys for our church.
5. I enjoy visiting countries and seeing the beauties of creation.
6. Carl's favorite activities are working with his two hobbies
7. We should pray and bring our worries to the Lord.

cherries   monkeys   butter flies

Page 94

Purpose

To review how to change words ending in **f** or **fe** into plural words.

To review making other words plural.

Lesson

Discuss the directions, noticing the words that are exceptions to the rule.

Carefully discuss the lesson with your student and have him answer orally before he completes the work independently.

Page 95

Purpose

To review how to change words ending with **o** into plural words.

To review how to make words plural by changing the words.

Lesson

Discuss the directions, noticing the words that are exceptions to the rule.

Discuss the lesson with your student and have him answer orally before he completes the work independently.

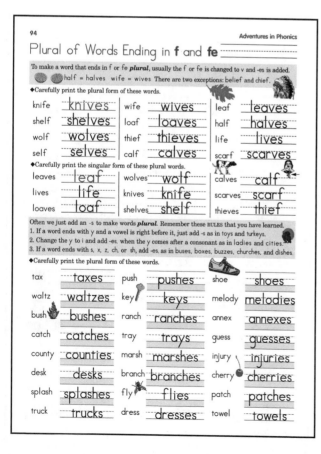

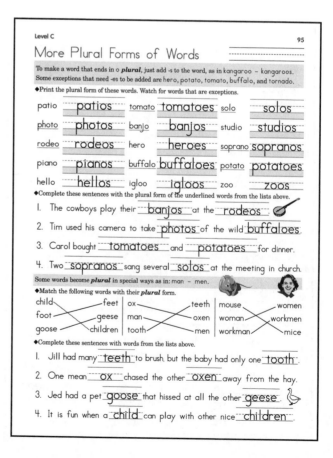

Page 96

Purpose

To review words that are spelled the same whether they are singular or plural.

To review how to change words that end with **f** or **fe** into plural words.

To review how to make words plural by changing the words.

Lesson

For this lesson, listen as your student reads the top list of words which are pronounced and spelled the same whether they are singular or plural. The student may say:

```
popcorn ⇨ "lots of" popcorn
 honey ⇨ "lots of" honey
```

Carefully discuss the lesson with your student, having him answer orally before he completes the work independently.

Note: The answers for sentences 1, 4, 7, 8, and 9 on page 96 may vary in the order in which the words are printed.

Page 97

Purpose

To review the plural forms of words.

Lesson

Discuss the five rules in the directions of the lesson.

After going over the lesson, have the student complete it independently.

Note: The first answer in sentence 1 on page 97 is *boys* but may also be *children*; likewise, the second answer in sentence 6 is *children* but may also be *boys*.

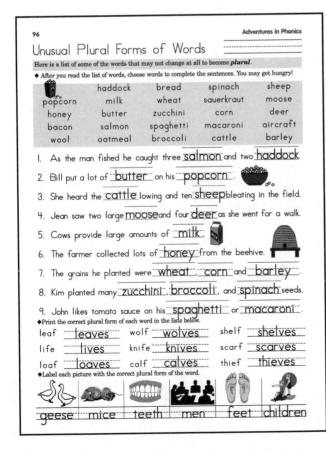

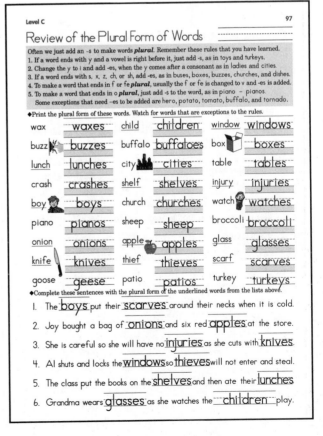

Page 98

Purpose

To reinforce the use and meaning of these prefixes.

Lesson

Discuss the rules at the top of the lesson.

When the student has a good understanding, have him answer orally before he completes the page independently.

Page 99

Purpose

To reinforce the use and meaning of these prefixes.

Lesson

Discuss the rules at the top of the lesson. Talk about the meaning of the words as they are read.

When the student has a good understanding, have him answer orally before he completes the page independently.

---

98   Adventures in Phonics

Prefixes **un- dis- non- ir- im- in- il-**

You have learned that *suffixes* are letters that are added to the **end** of a word to change or modify its meaning. -er -est -ed -ing -y -ful -less -ly -en -able -age -ance -ity -ive -ion
Prefixes are letters that are added to the **beginning** of a word to change or modify its meaning.
A suffix or prefix is a **syllable** in itself if it has a vowel sound, as in plant–ed or re–plant–ed.
Prefixes un-, dis-, non-, ir-, im-, in-, and il-, usually make the root word have the opposite meaning.

◆Underline the prefixes and print the root words on the lines.

unknown	known	incorrect	correct	illiterate	literate
dislike	like	displease	please	unpack	pack
nonsense	sense	irreverent	reverent	disobey	obey
unsafe	safe	nonstop	stop	impolite	polite
illegal	legal	impure	pure	insecure	secure
unkind	kind	indirect	direct	unfair	fair

◆Complete these sentences with words from the lists above.

1. One who can read is literate, but he who cannot is __illiterate__

2. It was __unsafe__ to drink the __impure__ water from the stream.

3. A good child would never __displease__ or __disobey__ his parents.

4. A rude person is usually __impolite__ when he speaks to people.

◆Match the words that are opposite in meaning. These are called **antonyms**.

mature	irregular	screw	dislocate	honest	unhappy
regular	unopened	locate	unwrap	happy	impure
patient	incapable	curable	disagree	comfort	dishonest
opened	impatient	appear	unscrew	pure	unfold
direct	disorder	wrap	incurable	legal	discomfort
capable	immature	certain	disappear	fold	unwilling
order	indirect	agree	uncertain	willing	illegal

Level C   99

Prefixes **in- en- im- em- mis-**

Prefixes in-, en-, im-, and em-, can have the meaning of *on* or *in*. inject encamp imprint embrace
The prefix mis- can mean *wrong, bad,* or *lack of.* misplace mistrust

◆Circle the prefixes in these words. Divide the words into syllables as you print them on the line.

misprint	mis–print	misplace	mis–place	inflate	in–flate
income	in–come	enclose	en–close	encircle	en–circle
misread	mis–read	mistrust	mis–trust	imprint	im–print
embrace	em–brace	impress	im–press	mislead	mis–lead
misdeed	mis–deed	misjudge	mis–judge	employ	em–ploy
increase	in–crease	embark	em–bark	mistreat	mis–treat

◆Use words from the lists above to complete the definitions. Some words may be new to you.

to read incorrectly	misread	to make a circle around	encircle
an error in printing	misprint	to surround or shut in	enclose
to judge wrongly	misjudge	to press or leave a mark	imprint
a wrong or wicked act	misdeed	to get greater in size	inflate
to treat wrongly	mistreat	to lead in the wrong way	mislead
to lovingly hold in arms	embrace	to receive or earn money	income

◆Match the definitions to the words.

to use something incorrectly	misspell	to make it better	indwell
an error in a trial	misuse	to be made part of	improve
an incorrect spelling	entrap	to dwell or live in	infect
to catch in a trap	mistrial	to cause a disease	involve
to put on a throne	import	to put aboard ship	implant
to make a slave	enthrone	to plant firmly or deeply	misbehave
to make larger	enslave	incorrect, error	embark
to bring into a country	enlarge	wrong behavior or action	mistake

Page 100

Purpose

To review the prefixes **a-** and **be-**.

Lesson

Discuss the rules at the top of the lesson.

After you have discussed the lesson and you feel that the student has a good understanding, have him answer orally before he completes the page independently.

Page 101

Purpose

To review the prefixes **de-** and **pre-**.

Lesson

Discuss the rules at the top of the lesson.

After you have discussed the lesson and you feel that the student has a good understanding, have him answer orally before he completes the page independently.

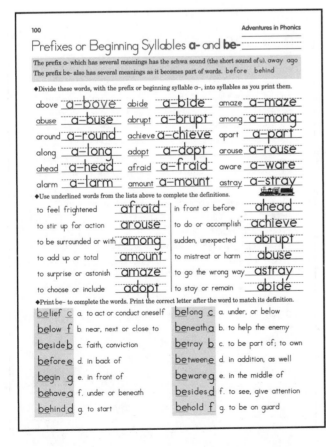

Page 102

Purpose

To review the prefixes **re-** and **ex-**.

Lesson

Discuss the rules at the top of the lesson.

After the student has a good understanding, listen as he answers orally, then have him complete the page independently.

Page 103

Purpose

To review the prefixes **fore-** and **for-**.

Lesson

Discuss the rules at the top of the lesson.

When the student has a good understanding, have him answer orally before he completes the page independently.

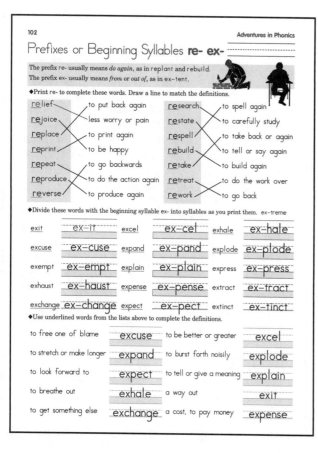

102 Adventures in Phonics

Prefixes or Beginning Syllables **re- ex-**

The prefix re- usually means *do again*, as in replant and rebuild.
The prefix ex- usually means *from* or *out of*, as in ex-tent.

◆Print re- to complete these words. Draw a line to match the definitions.

relief — less worry or pain
rejoice — to be happy
replace — to put back again
reprint — to print again
repeat — to do the action again
reproduce — to produce again
reverse — to go backwards

research — to carefully study
restate — to tell or say again
respell — to spell again
rebuild — to build again
retake — to take back or again
retreat — to go back
rework — to do the work over

◆Divide these words with the beginning syllable ex- into syllables as you print them. ex-treme

exit	ex-it	excel	ex-cel	exhale	ex-hale
excuse	ex-cuse	expand	ex-pand	explode	ex-plode
exempt	ex-empt	explain	ex-plain	express	ex-press
exhaust	ex-haust	expense	ex-pense	extract	ex-tract
exchange	ex-change	expect	ex-pect	extinct	ex-tinct

◆Use underlined words from the lists above to complete the definitions.

to free one of blame — excuse
to stretch or make longer — expand
to look forward to — expect
to breathe out — exhale
to get something else — exchange

to be better or greater — excel
to burst forth noisily — explode
to tell or give a meaning — explain
a way out — exit
a cost, to pay money — expense

Level C 103

Prefixes or Beginning Syllables **fore- for-**

The prefix fore- usually means *before* in time and place, as in forefathers.
The prefix for- usually means *away, apart,* or *off*, as in forbid.

◆Print the prefix fore- to complete these words. Draw a line to match the definitions.

forecast — a prediction, warning
forefront — the extreme front
foregone — that has gone before
forearm — arm from wrist to elbow
foreclose — to legally end a mortgage
forefather — an ancestor
forefoot — front foot of an animal

forehead — face just below hairline
foreground — scene nearest viewer
forefinger — finger nearest thumb
foresee — to see beforehand
forenoon — time from sunrise to noon
foretell — to suggest beforehand
forewarn — to warn beforehand

◆Divide these words with the beginning syllable for- into syllables as you print them.

forsake	for-sake	forgo	for-go	forbid	for-bid
forget	for-get	forlorn	for-lorn	forever	for-ev-er
forgive	for-give	forward	for-ward	forfeit	for-feit

The word *forgo* means "to give up" or "to let pass." *Forlorn* means "deserted" or "without hope."

◆Use words from the lists above to complete the following definitions.

to remember no more — forget
left behind, deserted — forlorn
to pardon, to overlook — forgive

for eternity, for always — forever
to rule against, prevent — forbid
to move ahead, advance — forward

◆Complete these sentences with words from the lists in the middle of the page.

1. In the Lord's Prayer we ask God to forgive our sins as we forgive others.
2. The Lord will never leave or forsake His people.
3. Christians will live with the Lord in heaven forever.
4. The band played cheerful music as it marched forward through the town.
5. It is for Tim's safety that his parents forbid him to play near the road.

Page 104

Purpose
To review suffixes and prefixes.

Lesson
Discuss the rules at the top of the lesson.

After the student has answered orally, have him complete the page independently.

Page 105

Purpose
To review the first four rules for dividing words into syllables.

Lesson
Discuss the four rules in this lesson and have your student explain orally how to divide a few of the words under each rule.

When the student has a good understanding of the rules, have him do the work by himself.

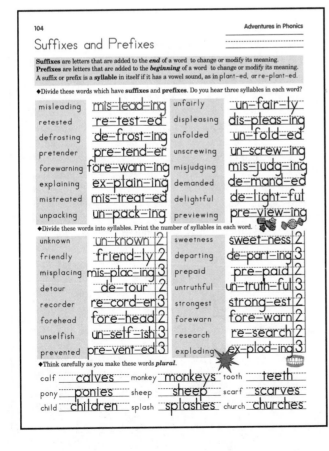

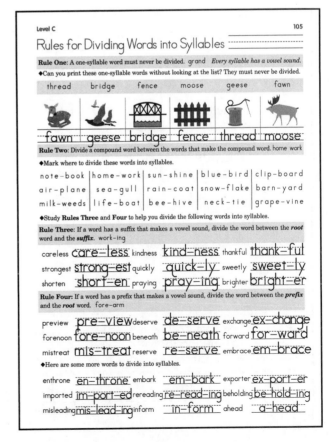

Page 106

Purpose

To review Rule Five for dividing syllables, working especially with words that have double consonants.

Lesson

As you discuss this rule, reinforce that in words having short vowel sounds, a consonant follows that vowel sound. Use the chart below for examples.

ar•row	bon•net	pep•per
bag•gage	hap•pen	pop•py
bat•ter	hol•low	rib•bon
bet•ter	mot•to	skil•let

Discuss the fact that, in root words ending with the double letters **ff**, **ll**, **ss**, and **zz**, *these double letters must not be divided.*

stuff•ing, call•er

glass•es, buzz•ing

Carefully go over the lesson and listen as your student answers orally before he does the work by himself.

Note: Rule Ten (*see pages 118 and 119 in the workbook*) is cited in this lesson because words ending with **le** appear in the exercise below where the rule is mentioned.

Page 107

Purpose

To review Rule Five for dividing syllables, working with words having two different consonants in the middle.

Lesson

As you review this rule written on the top of the page, use the words in the following chart.

ac•tion	win•ter	pow•der
vel•vet	shoul•der	plas•ter
pub•lic	sher•bert	pew•ter
trum•pet	ser•mon	par•ty
splin•ter	pul•pit	don•key

After you carefully go over the lesson and listen as your student answers orally, have him do the work by himself.

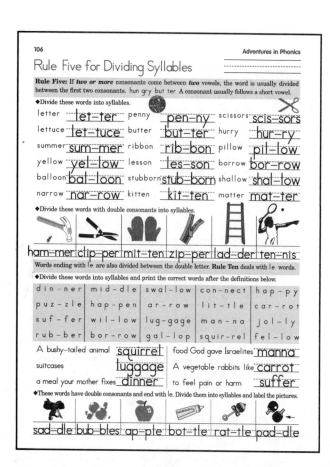

Page 108

Purpose

To reinforce Rule Five for dividing words into syllables.

Lesson

Go over the previous lesson. Review this rule along with **Rule Three** on page 105 of the workbook, discussing words with suffixes. Ask your student to divide the words on the chart below:

call–ing	hap–py	buzz–er
fel–low	clap–ping	hop–ping
stuff–ing	dress–er	glass–es
let–ter	pass–ing	run–ning
let–ting	fun–ny	full–est

When your student understands this rule, and has carefully gone over the lesson giving his answers orally, have him do the work by himself.

Page 109

Purpose

To review the first five rules for dividing words into syllables.

Lesson

Thoroughly discuss each rule. Spend as much time as necessary to help your student understand.

Carefully go over the list of words and listen as he answers orally before he does the work by himself.

Page 110

Purpose

To review Rule Six for dividing words into syllables.

Lesson

As you review this rule, the student again needs to listen for the vowel sounds, remembering that a **short vowel sound** is usually followed by a consonant or a consonant digraph. Give as much help and time as needed. Ask the student to divide the following words:

rob•in	shad•ow	gath•er
moth•er	tim•id	fam•ine
heav•en	sliv•er	buck•et

When your student understands this rule, carefully go over the lesson and listen as he answers orally before he does the work by himself.

Page 111

Purpose

To reinforce Rule Six for dividing words into syllables.

Lesson

Thoroughly review Rule Six at the top of the lesson with your student. Suggest that he looks back at the previous lesson. Give as much help and time as needed.

When you think that he understands this rule, carefully go over the lesson and listen as he answers orally before he does the work by himself.

As it is suggested for all of the lessons, correct his work the same day it is completed, talk about any errors, and have them corrected right away.

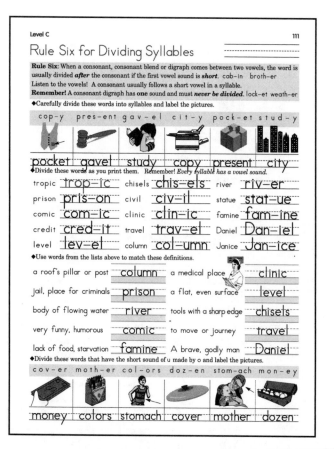

Page 112

Purpose

To review Rule Seven for dividing words into syllables.

Lesson

Review the previous lesson about Rule Six. As you discuss Rule Seven, the student again needs to listen for the vowel sounds, remembering that a **long vowel sound** can be at the end of a word or syllable. A vowel digraph (**ay**, **ea**, etc.) must not be divided, as it makes the long vowel sound. Give as much help and time as needed. Ask the student to divide the following words:

pa•per	rea•son	se•cret
pro•vide	bea•ver	so•lo
ra•dar	sa•cred	su•per

There are usually a few exceptions to rules. One exception for this rule is **sen•ior**.

When your student has a good understanding of the lesson and has gone over the answers orally, have him print the lesson.

Page 113

Purpose

To reinforce Rule Seven for dividing words into syllables.

Lesson

Looking back on the previous lesson may be helpful. Give as much help and time as needed while you discuss this lesson.

When your student understands this rule and has given the answers orally, have him complete the lesson in pencil.

Note: The last word (*crayons*) in the word list at the top of page 113 does not follow the rule emphasized in this lesson.

The rule stressed on this page is as follows:

When a consonant, consonant blend, or digraph comes between *two* vowels, the word is usually divided *before* the consonant if the first vowel sound is *long*.

However, the word *crayons* (crāy'ŏns) is divided before a vowel. Also, the letter *y* is used as a vowel that makes the *a* long, so there are actually three vowels in a row, and the word divided between them. (This may be said to follow Rule Nine, which is introduced on workbook page 116.)

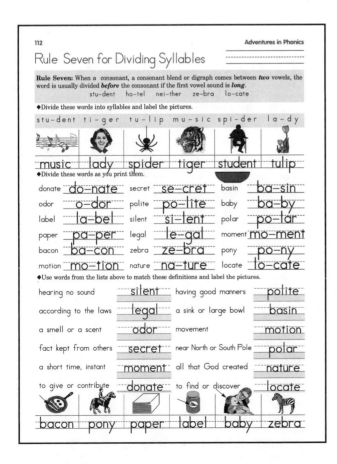

Page 114

Purpose

To review Rules Six and Seven for dividing words into syllables.

Lesson

Review the rules in this lesson one at a time, using the words in the sections as examples.

When the lesson has been answered orally, have the student complete it independently.

Page 115

Purpose

To review Rule Eight for dividing words into syllables.

Lesson

Carefully discuss this rule. Give as much help and time as needed. Study the following list of words as examples:

o•pen	e•vent	hol•i•day
o•ver	e•qual	A•pril
o•cean	po•li•o	i•ron

When the student understands this rule and has given the answers orally, have him complete the lesson in pencil.

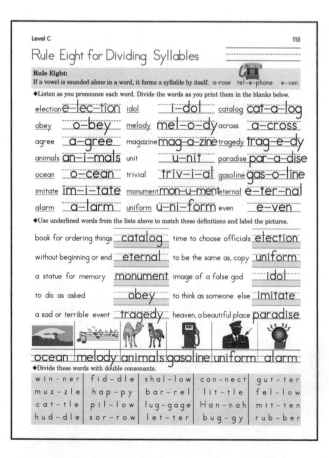

Page 116

Purpose

To review Rule Nine for dividing words into syllables.

To review how to change words ending with y into plural words.

Lesson

Carefully discuss this rule. Study the following lists of words as examples:

qui•et	flu•id	di•al
tri•al	cre•ate	po•em
di•et	li•on	di•a•per*

*Certain dictionaries divide the word *diaper* into two syllables: dia•per.

Take as much time as necessary to teach these more difficult lessons.

When your student has a good understanding of the page and has given the answers orally, have him complete the lesson in pencil.

Page 117

Purpose

To reinforce Rules Eight and Nine for dividing words into syllables.

Lesson

Discuss these two rules. Give as much time and help as needed.

When your student has given the answers orally and has a good understanding of the page, have him complete the lesson in pencil.

116   Adventures in Phonics

Rule Nine for Dividing Syllables

Rule Nine:
When *two* vowels come together and are sounded separately, divide the word between the two vowels, as in po-et, ri-ot, and pi-a-no.

◆Carefully divide these words. You may also need to remember other RULES along with **Rule Nine**.

violet vi-o-let	ruin ru-in	violin vi-o-lin
giant gi-ant	create cre-ate	poem po-em
cruel cru-el	lion li-on	science sci-ence
radio ra-di-o	rodeo ro-de-o	fuel fu-el
diaper di-a-per	quiet qui-et	bias bi-as
annual an-nu-al	usual u-su-al	fluid flu-id
idea i-de-a	diet di-et	poet po-et

◆Use the words from the lists above to match these definitions and label the pictures below.

a liquid that can flow	fluid	a small plant, purple color	violet
one who writes poetry	poet	to damage, destroy	ruin
without any noise	quiet	brutal, causing pain	cruel
yearly, a year's time	annual	of a great size	giant
a mental thought, opinion	idea	food or drink that is eaten	diet
to make, bring into being	create	something burned for heat	fuel

radio   lion   violin   poem   science   rodeo

◆How do you make these words ending with y plural?

cherry cherries	monkey monkeys	county counties
pony ponies	daisy daisies	berry berries
donkey donkeys	joy joys	delay delays

Level C   117

Review of Rules Eight and Nine

Rule Eight:
If a vowel is sounded alone in a word, it forms a syllable by itself, as in a-rose and e-ven.

Rule Nine:
When *two* vowels come together and are sounded separately, divide the word between the two vowels, as in po-et, ri-ot, and pi-a-no.

◆Carefully listen for the syllables as you divide the words. Remember all RULES as you work.

uniform u-ni-form	melody met-o-dy	piano pi-a-no
violin vi-o-lin	science sci-ence	radio ra-di-o
enough e-nough	monument mon-u-ment	glorified glo-ri-fied
catalog cat-a-log	quiet qui-et	create cre-ate
annual an-nu-al	giant gi-ant	open o-pen
gasoline gas-o-line	telephone tel-e-phone	eternal e-ter-nal
around a-round	animals an-i-mals	even e-ven

◆Complete the following sentences with the underlined words above, dividing them *only* where they come at the end of a line.

Why should we know about syllables? Sometimes there is not enough space on the line for the whole word.

1. Mr. Sherman began taking pian-o lessons when he was very young.

2. He thought he had practiced e-nough when the sun would shine.

3. On sunny days he liked to run a-round with his friends.

4. He worked hard to learn the mel-ody of each song he was given.

5. First he began to study the vi-olin, but he did not do well.

6. He was asked to play the piano e-ven while he was in the Navy.

7. As he played he wore his Navy u-niform.

8. Mr. Sherman hoped his music glo-rified His precious Lord.

◆Print the plural form of these words.

child children	goose geese	woman women
tooth teeth	mouse mice	workman workmen
	foot feet	ox oxen

Page 118

Purpose
To reinforce Rule Ten-a for dividing words into syllables.

Lesson
Discuss this rule which works with words ending in **le**. Think about the vowel sounds in the first syllable.

A short vowel needs a consonant.

dimple candle gentle

A long vowel can stand alone.

table eagle maple

When your student has a good understanding of the page, have him complete the lesson in pencil.

Page 119

Purpose
To reinforce Rule Ten-b for dividing words into syllables.

Lesson
Discuss this rule which works with words ending in **ckle**. Think about the vowel sounds in the first syllable. Notice that these words have short vowel sounds. The consonant digraph **ck** belongs with the short vowel sound.

pick–le buck–le tack–le

When your student has given the answers orally and has a good understanding of the page, have him print the answers.

---

118   Adventures in Phonics

Rule Ten–a for Dividing Syllables

Rule Ten a: If a word ends in l e, the consonant before the l e is usually part of the last syllable, and the e has the *schwa* (ə) sound. ta ble   tum ble   *Every syllable has a vowel sound.*

◆Carefully divide these words. Remember that the l e needs a consonant in these words.

gen–tle	bat–tle	bu–gle	sad–dle	cra–dle
nib–ble	ap–ple	lit–tle	an–kle	hum–ble
scrib–ble	rat–tle	pad–dle	ket–tle	stum–ble
ma–ple	peo–ple	rip–ple	set–tle	grum–ble
ta–ble	driz–zle	bun–dle	med–dle	fum–ble
sta–ple	can–dle	gig–gle	fid–dle	tum–ble
la–dle	tur–tle	wig–gle	mid–dle	jum–ble
this–tle	ea–gle	sprin–kle	dim–ples	pud–dle
whis–tle	bea–gle	twin–kle	sim–ple	mar–bles

◆Complete these sentences with the underlined words from the lists above.

1. Scott wore his boots and enjoyed walking in a **puddle** after the storm.
2. Jeff and Lisa were happy that so many **people** came to their wedding.
3. Emmy's new **little** puppy likes to chew or **nibble** on her shoes.
4. Lonna has cute, little **dimples** on her cheeks.
5. Mrs. Smith made us delicious tea in her **kettle**.
6. The boys sat in the **middle** of the floor and played with **marbles**.
7. We heard the silly, little girls **giggle** as they would wiggle in their beds.
8. Dan helped his father **bundle** sticks and **sprinkle** the lawn.

◆Label these pictures with the underlined words from the lists above.   sta ple   pad dle

| cradle | saddle | paddle | bugle | candle | table |

Level C   119

Rule Ten–b for Dividing Syllables

Rule Ten b:
If a word ends in ckle, the l e stands alone. The consonant digraph ck must never be divided and must stay with the short vowel in the first syllable: tack le   pick le.

◆Carefully divide these words. The l e stands alone because the ck stays with the short vowel.

cack–le	shack–le	heck–le	tick–le	
tack–le	freck–les	sick–le	prick–le	buck–le
crack–le	speck–le	pick–les	trick–le	chuck–le

◆Complete these sentences with words from the lists above.

1. A slow **trickle** of water dripped from the leaky faucet.
2. The fire made a **crackle** sound as it burned the sticks.
3. We could hear the hens **cackle** in the chicken coop.
4. We heard the baby giggle as his father would **tickle** him.
5. The farmer used his **sickle** to cut the long grass.
6. It is not polite to pester or **heckle** someone as he speaks.
7. The boy with the **freckles** on his nose liked to eat **pickles**.

Rule Ten a: If a word ends in l e, the consonant before the l e is part of the last syllable. ta ble | **Rule Ten b:** If a word ends in ckle, the l e stands alone and ck stays with the short vowel: pick le.

◆Think about these RULES as you divide these words.

pad–dle	ruf–fle	buck–le	tur–tle
mid–dle	strug–gle	thim–ble	stee–ple
pick–le	sick–le	snug–gle	tick–le
bu–gle	tack–le	tum–ble	dim–ple
pur–ple	ca–ble	bicy–cle	bun–dle
sin–gle	twin–kle	chuck–le	wres–tle
crack–le	spar–kle	pud–dle	ket–tle

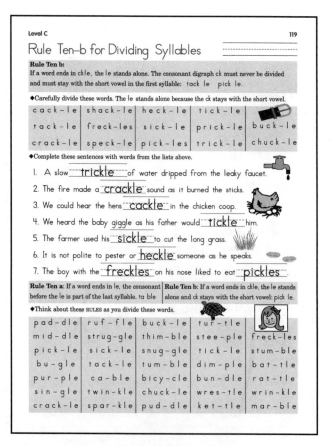

| freck–les |
| stum–ble |
| bat–tle |
| rat–tle |
| wrin–kle |
| mar–ble |

Page 120

Purpose

To explain the need to have accented syllables.

Lesson

Review the definition of a *syllable*.

A syllable is a word or part of a word with one vowel sound and is pronounced with a single sound of the voice.

hand   door   tree   straight

When a word has more than one syllable, one of the syllables is accented. Note the following words.

mas´•ter	moon´•light
not	*not*
mas•ter´	moon•light´
pre•tend´	cor•rect´
not	*not*
pre´•tend	cor´•rect

Take as much time as necessary to teach these more difficult lessons.

When your student understands the lesson, listen as he reads the words orally before he does the work by himself.

Page 121

Purpose

To help the student understand the value of using a dictionary.

To teach putting words into alphabetical order.

Lesson

Spend some time with your student looking through a dictionary. You may want to make a list of words which he could find in a dictionary and print the phonetic way to pronounce the words, or print the definition of the words.

Work slowly as you teach these lessons.

When your student understands this lesson, have him complete it independently.

---

120   Adventures in Phonics

Accented Syllables

As you read words with more than one syllable, you can hear that one syllable is pronounced with *emphasis*, or in a *stronger* and more *accented* way than the others. The accent mark follows the accented syllable. Notice the accented syllable as you say these words.

ac´ cent   ta´ ble   dis please´   thank´ ful   talk´ ing   Nan´ cy   un fold´ ing   joy´ ful   Jo´ seph

◆Read these words and put an *accent* mark (´) after the syllable that is *stronger* or said with force.

	pick´ le	ap´ ple	e´ ven	na´ tion
	ex tend´	kind´ ness	ev´ er	birth´ day
stu´ dent	bush´ el	gen´ tle	qui´ et	call´ ing
heav´ en	pen´ cil	e nough´	rob´ in	laugh´ ing
a wake´	help´ ful	a round´	pock´ et	mis treat´
chil´ dren	pre´ view	grum´ ble	dis please´	bal loon´
man´ ners	pan´ da	sci´ ence	thank´ ful	mail´ man

◆Read these names and put an accent mark (´) after the syllable that is *stronger* or said with force. Do you notice that the **first** syllable of each of these names is the **accented** syllable?

Han´ nah	Jo´ seph	Ab´ i gail	Mi´ chael	Ed´ ward
Jan´ et	Kel´ sey	Lon´ na	Da´ vid	Nan´ cy
Ra´ chel	Er´ ic	Cal´ vin	Swe´ den	Af´ ri ca
Pe´ ter	Con´ nel	Kar´ la	Nor´ way	Pil´ grim
Na´ than	Al´ i son	Kim´ ber ly	Can´ a da	Eng´ lish

Why does the name *Grace* not have an accented syllable? Never divide a one-syllable word!

◆As you label these pictures, put the accent mark after the syllable that is **emphasized** in each word.

li´ on	pan´ da	ti´ ger	lob´ster	spi´ der	star´fish
cab´ in	wind´ mill	mitt´ out	let	hot´ dog	pick´ le	tur´ tle

Level C   121

A Close Look at the Dictionary

As you may already know, a *dictionary* is a very helpful book to own and use. Our God is a God of order. Our lives also should have good order. One good way of order is to place books, words, etc. in the order of our alphabet. It is very important then that everyone knows not only the *vowel markings* and *sounds* of our alphabet, but also its *order*.

In a dictionary, the words of our language are arranged in alphabetical order. Definitions, pronunciation, and often other information are given for each word.

Spend some time get•ting ac•quaint•ed with one of these books.

◆Here is an example of how the top of a page in a dictionary for young students may look.

dictatorial	**digest**
dic•ta•to•ri•al (dik´ tə tôr´ ē əl), adj. of, like or characteristic of a dictator; autocratic; imperious, domineering.	**dif•fer•ence** (dif´ ər əns, dif´ rəns), n. 1. unlikeness between two or more persons or things, as, the difference between the dogs. 2.
dic•tion (dik´ shən), n. 1.manner of expression in words; choice of words. 2. enunciation.	The amount by which one number differs from another; the number that is obtained when one number is subtracted from another; as the difference between six and eight is two.
dic•tion•ar•y (dik´ shə när´ ē), n.1. a book of alphabetically listed words in a language, with definition, etymologies, pronunciation, etc.; 2. alphabetically arranged list of words relating to a special subject.	**dif•fer•en•tial** (dif´ ə ren´ shəl) n. A device which allows one rear wheel of a car to turn faster than the other, as in going around a curve.
dic•tum (dik´ təm), n. An authoritative state-	

◆Neatly print the lower case letters of the alphabet to be a guide for you.

a b c d e f g h i j k l m n o p q r s t u v w x y z

◆Put an *accent* mark (´) after the syllable that is *stronger* or said with force.

Alphabetize the group of words in each list by number. If you do not have words that begin with every letter in the alphabet, just skip to the next letter.

4	de scribe´	3	doc´ tor	2	in crease´
5	em´ pire	2	barn´ yard	3	mas´ ter
1	a´ ble	4	en´ gine	1	fid´ dler
3	cof´ fee	1	ad just´	5	un lock´
2	bap´ tize	5	grape´ fruit	4	pars´ ley

◆Put an *accent* mark (´) after the syllable that is *emphasized*. Alphabetize the group of words in each list by number. If words in each list begin with the same letter or letters, look at the next letter of each word.

3	po lice´	3	ram´ ble		de scribe´
1	neigh´ bor	2	rain´ bow	2	tim´ ber
4	pre vent´	1	raft´ er	4	un´ true
2	per´ son	4	re view	3	um´ pire

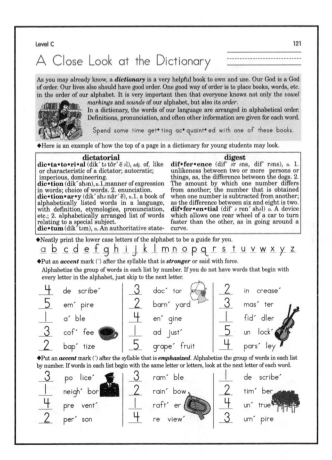

Page 122

Purpose
To review the proper use of accented syllables.

Lesson
Carefully go over the directions in the lesson. Take as much time as necessary to teach these lessons.

When your student understands this page, listen as he gives the answers orally before he does the work by himself.

Page 123

Purpose
To review the proper use of accented syllables.

Lesson
Discuss the previous lesson. Then carefully go over the directions for this lesson.

When your student understands this page, listen as he answers, before he completes the work by himself.

Note: The answer under the second image at the bottom of page 123 is *turtle*, but the word *puddle* is also possible.

122　　　　　　　　　　　　　　　　　　Adventures in Phonics

Accented Syllables and Pronunciation

As you read words with more than one syllable and pronounce the correct syllable with *emphasis*, you are reading with expression. Peoˊple should be thankˊful for evˊery blessˊing from the Lord. This lesson deals with pronunciation marks which help us read words.

◆Mark the accented syllables (ˊ) in all lists. Match each word to the way it may be pronounced.

	harˊ nis	hard en	mŏnˊ strəs	mon key
ĕnˊ jin	en er gize	hardˊ lē	har poon	mōˊ mənt	mon ey
ĕn fôrsˊ	en gine	harˊ dˊn	har vest	mŭnˊ ē	mo ment
ĕnˊ er jīzˊ	en grave	har pōōnˊ	har mo ny	mŭngˊ kē	Mon day
ĕn grāvˊ	en close	harˊ mə nē	har ness	môrˊ ning	mon strous
ĕn klōzˊ	en force	harˊ vestˊ	hard ly	Mŭnˊ dā	morn ing

◆Mark the accented syllables (ˊ) in all lists. Match each word to the way it may be pronounced.

iks chănjˊ	ex am ple	nōˊ ing	knit ting	rĭgˊ əl	wres tle
ĕkˊ ser sīz	ex cel lent	nŭkˊ əl	knowl edge	rĭtˊ ing	wrap per
ik splănˊ	ex change	nŏlˊ ij	knuck le	răpˊ ər	wreck age
ĕkˊ sə lənt	ex cept	nŏtˊ hōl	knap sack	rĕkˊ ij	wrin kle
ig zamˊ pəl	ex er cise	năpˊ săk	knot hole	rĕsˊ əl	wrig gle
ik septˊ	ex plain	nĭtˊ ing	know ing	rĭngˊ kəl	writ ing

◆Put an *accent* mark (ˊ) after the syllable that is *emphasized*. Alphabetize the group of words in each list by number. Since words in each list begin with the same letter or letters, look at the next letter(s) of each word.

3	Scripˊ ture	1	tarˊ nish	2	yelˊ low
1	sandˊ box	3	temˊ per	1	yardˊ stick
4	seˊ cret	2	teaˊ pot	4	youthˊ ful
5	selfˊ ish	5	thornˊ y	3	yieldˊ ing
2	scisˊ sors	4	thirˊ ty	5	yucˊ ca

◆Label these pictures with words from the lists above.

thirty　Scripture　thorny　youthful　scissors　teapot

Level C　　　　　　　　　　　　　　　　　　　　　123

Accented Syllables and Pronunciation

It can be tiring to hear people read without expression. They may sound like a robot talking. It is important to pronounce the correct syllable with *emphasis*. Remember that the sign ə stands for the short sound of u. A gosˊsip beˊtrays a conˊfiˊdence, but a trustˊworˊthy man keeps a seˊcret.

◆Mark the vowels in the first syllables, mark the accented syllables (ˊ), and match the words.

	kôˊ shən	no tion	ə dŏpˊ shən	af fec tion
nāˊ shən	sta tion	lōˊ shən	ac tion	dŏ nāˊ shən	ad di tion
mōˊ shən	na tion	frăkˊ shən	cau tion	ə dĭshˊ ən	ed u ca tion
mĕnˊ shən	fic tion	nōˊ shən	e lec tion	vā kāˊ shən	a dop tion
stāˊ shən	mo tion	ăkˊ shən	frac tion	ə fĕkˊ shən	va ca tion
fĭkˊ shən	men tion	ĭ lĕkˊ shən	lo tion	ĕj ŏŏ kāˊ shən	do na tion

◆It is easy and fun when you know your markings for the sounds. Here are some more to do.

nāˊ chər	ma ture	băkˊ ward	in ward	lŭgˊ ij	o pin ion
ădˊ ven chər	na ture	fôrˊ ward	out ward	pärˊ shəl	lug gage
lĕkˊ chər	pas ture	ĭnˊ ward	back ward	frĕndˊ ship	par tial
fāˊ chər	lec ture	outˊ ward	up ward	ə pĭnˊ yən	post age
mə chŏŏrˊ	ad ven ture	ŭpˊ ward	down ward	ôrˊ gə nīz	friend ship
păsˊ chər	fea ture	downˊ ward	for ward	pōˊ stij	or gan ize

◆Put an *accent* mark (ˊ) after the syllable that is *emphasized*. Alphabetize the group of words in each list by number. If words in each list begin with the same letter or letters, look at the next letter of each word.

1	canˊ dle	2	pudˊ dle	3	shufˊ fle
3	padˊ dle	4	ratˊ tle	5	triˊ an gle
5	turˊ tle	1	fumˊ ble	1	anˊ kle
4	ridˊ dle	5	sparˊ kle	4	thimˊ ble
2	humˊ ble	3	purˊ ple	2	fidˊ dle

◆Label these pictures with words from the lists above.

thimble　turtle　sparkle　paddle　triangle　candle

Page 124

Purpose

To reinforce the first five rules for dividing words into syllables.

Lesson

Spend enough time discussing these rules again. Carefully go over the rules and directions on the lesson.

When your student understands these rules, listen as he gives the answers orally before he does the work by himself.

Note: On workbook page 124 below, the word *miscount* is marked as a *verb* with an accent on the second syllable (mis•count'); as a *noun*, however, the accent would be on the first syllable (mis'count).

Page 125

Purpose

To reinforce Rules Six, Seven, Eight, and Nine for dividing words into syllables.

Lesson

Discuss these four rules again. Carefully go over the lesson. Encourage careful, small printing so the words will fit in the space.

When the student has a good understanding, listen as he gives the answers orally before he does the lesson.

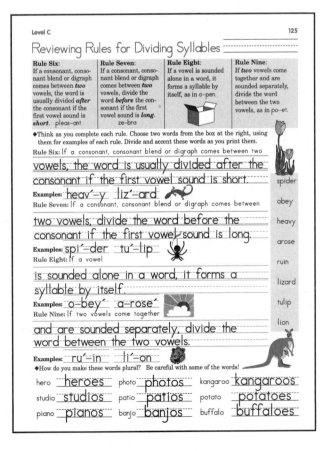

Page 126

Purpose

To give extra review of Rule Ten.

To give additional work with accented syllables and alphabetizing.

Lesson

Carefully go over the rules and directions in the lesson with your student.

When he has a good understanding, listen as he reads the words orally before he does the work by himself.

Page 127

Purpose

To give additional work with Rule Ten.

To have the student do more work with accents and alphabetizing.

Lesson

Review the rules and directions in the lesson with your student.

When he has a good understanding, listen as he reads the words orally before he does the work by himself.

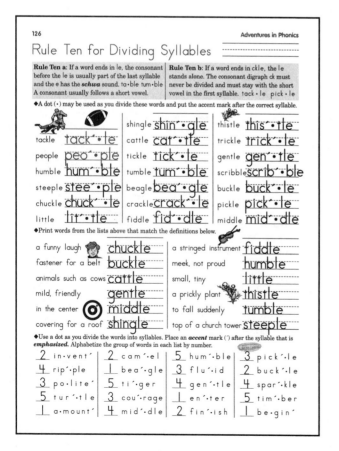

Page 128

Purpose

To review the sounds the vowel **a** can make.

To review the three sounds made by the suffix **-ed**.

Lesson

Carefully go over the rules and directions in the lesson with your student. Take as much time as necessary as you teach these lessons.

When he has a good understanding, listen as he reads the words orally before he does the work by himself.

Page 129

Purpose

To review the sounds the vowel **o** can make.

To review the two sounds made by **oo**.

Lesson

Discuss the rules and directions in the lesson with your student. Take as much time as necessary as you teach these lessons.

Before he does the work by himself, listen as he explains the answers orally.

Note: The word *hooves* in the middle of page 129 may be marked either as hŏŏves or hōōves.

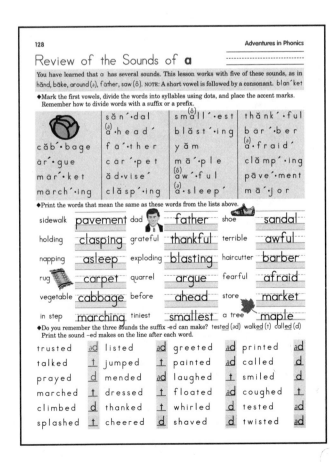

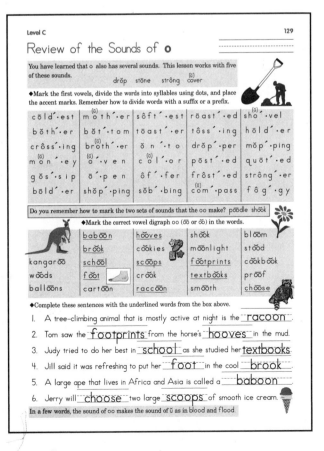

Page 130

Purpose

To review the several sounds made by **ou**.

Lesson

Carefully go over the rules and directions in the lesson with your student. Help him to distinguish between the different sounds. Take as much time as necessary as you teach these more difficult lessons.

When your student has a good understanding, listen as he gives the answers orally before he does the work by himself.

Note: The first two vowels in the word *bouquet* (found in the middle of page 130) may be marked either as bōō•quet′ or bo͝u•quet′ with the accent on the second syllable in both cases.

Page 131

Purpose

To review the several sounds made by **ou**.

Lesson

Carefully go over the lesson with your student, taking as much time as necessary to teach these lessons.

When your student has a good understanding and has given the answers orally, have him complete the work by himself.

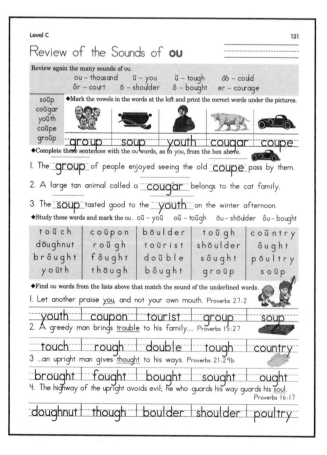

Page 132

Purpose
To review words with these sounds.

Lesson
Explain the sound these letters make. (**sh** or **zh**)

Listen as your student reads the following words:

precious	vision	nation
special	mission	action
social	passion	patient
vicious	mansion	cautious
ancient	pension	station

When your student seems to understand the lesson, listen as he gives the answers orally before he does the work by himself.

Page 133

Purpose
To help the student easily read words with these sounds.

Lesson
Review the sounds the following letters make: **ci, si, ti, sure,** and **ture.**

Encourage your student to read the following words until he knows them well:

precious	confusion	pleasure
special	addition	nature
ancient	caption	creature
television	measure	picture
division	treasure	future

Carefully go over the lesson until your student has a good understanding. Listen as he gives the answers orally before he completes the work independently.

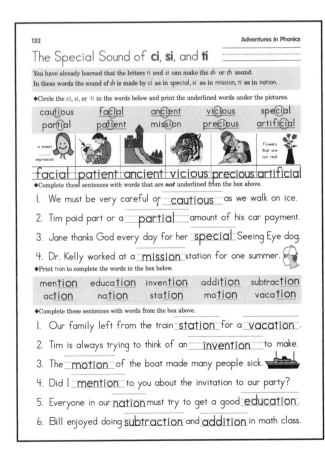

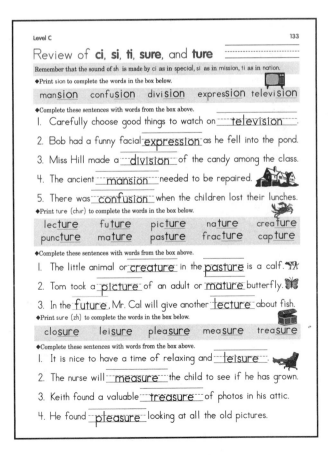

Page 134

Purpose

To review rules for making words plural.

Lesson

A quick look back to the previous two lessons would be good for review.

Discuss the rules at the top of this lesson.

When the student understands the page and has given the answers orally, have him do the work by himself.

Page 135

Purpose

To review rules for making words plural.

Lesson

Before discussing this page, review the previous lesson. Was the printing done neatly? Were there many mistakes?

Talk about the rules of this new lesson, especially the exceptions.

After the student has given the answers orally, have him complete the work independently.

134   Adventures in Phonics

Review of Plural Words

Often we just add an -s to make words plural. Remember these RULES that you have learned.
1. If a word ends with y and a vowel is right before it, just add -s as in toys and turkeys.
2. Change the y to i and add -es, when the y comes after a consonant as in ladies and cities.
3. If a word ends with s, x, z, ch, or sh, add -es, as in buses, boxes, buzzes, churches, and dishes.

◆Add -s to these words to make them plural.   book crayon egg stick towel banana

books crayons eggs sticks towels bananas

◆1. If a word ends in y and a vowel is right before it, just add -s. Make these words plural.
toy turkey key boy tray donkey

toys turkeys keys boys trays donkeys

◆2. Change the y to i and add -es, when the y comes after a consonant as in ladies and cities.
Think of the RULES as you make these words plural. Does a vowel or consonant come before the y?

puppy	puppies	duty	duties	berry	berries
turkey	turkeys	candy	candies	daisy	daisies
county	counties	copy	copies	valley	valleys
study	studies	monkey	monkeys	baby	babies
display	displays	pony	ponies	lady	ladies

◆3. If a word ends with s, x, z, ch, or sh, add -es, as in buses, boxes, buzzes, churches, and dishes.

Add the correct suffix (-s or -es) to make these words plural.

switch**es**	tray**s**	truck**s**	lion**s**
couch**es**	cross**es**	ash**es**	branch**es**
stamp**s**	comb**s**	swing**s**	wasp**s**
bush**es**	porch**es**	match**es**	wish**es**
beach**es**	bench**es**	hand**s**	fox**es**
	kiss**es**	block**s**	stone**s**
	wax**es**	ax**es**	lunch**es**

Level C   135

Review of Plural Words

To make a word that ends in f or fe **plural**, usually the f or fe is changed to v and -es is added.
half = halves wife = wives   There are two exceptions: belief and chief.

◆Carefully make these words plural.

knife	knives	wife	wives	leaf	leaves
shelf	shelves	loaf	loaves	half	halves
wolf	wolves	thief	thieves	life	lives
self	selves	calf	calves	scarf	scarves

To make a word that ends in o **plural**, just add -s to the word as in piano – pianos.
Some exceptions that need -es to be added are hero, potato, tomato, buffalo, and tornado.

◆Carefully make these words plural. Watch for the exceptions.

patio	patios	tomato	tomatoes	banjo	banjos
photo	photos	hero	heroes	solo	solos
rodeo	rodeos	avocado	avocados	studio	studios
piano	pianos	buffalo	buffaloes	soprano	sopranos
tornado	tornadoes	igloo	igloos	kangaroo	kangaroos
hello	hellos	zoo	zoos	potato	potatoes

Some words become **plural** in special ways.   man – men

◆Carefully make these words plural.

child	children	mouse	mice	woman	women
foot	feet	workman	workmen	man	men
goose	geese	ox	oxen	tooth	teeth

Here is a list of some of the words that may not change at all to become **plural**.

Read them as you say "**lots of**" ...

chili	salmon	zucchini	corn
popcorn	haddock	oatmeal	spaghetti	sauerkraut
honey	milk	bread	broccoli	macaroni
bacon	butter	wheat	spinach	cattle

Page 136

Purpose
To teach the use of the apostrophe for possessive words.

Lesson
Carefully discuss with your student the rules for using the apostrophe.

Have him read the following examples of using the apostrophe for possession:

Tom has a dog.
It is Tom's dog.

Jan has a coat.
It is Jan's coat.

A cow has a bell.
It is the cow's bell.

When your student understands the page and has given the answers orally, have him do the lesson independently.

Page 137

Purpose
To spend more time learning about the apostrophe with possessive words.

Lesson
It may be a little difficult to understand where to use the apostrophe with singular and plural words. Therefore, thoroughly go over the explanations under Rule 1 at the top of the lesson.

For extra practice, discuss the examples below. Before putting an apostrophe mark or an s anywhere; *first print the singular or plural form of the word,* then make it possessive.

a lady's hats	⇨ six ladies' hats
a tree's leaves	⇨ the trees' leaves
a man's coats	⇨ the men's coats
a cat's paws	⇨ the cats' paws
a baby's bibs	⇨ the babies' bibs
wolf's den	⇨ wolves' den

After your student understands the page and has given the answers orally, have him do the work independently.

---

136   Adventures in Phonics

The Apostrophe for Possession

The small mark called the **apostrophe** (') is used in two ways. This lesson deals with the first way.
Rule 1: To show that someone or something owns or possesses something, usually an **apostrophe** and **s** ('s) are added to the end of the word. (Rule 2, concerning contractions, is covered in a later lesson.)
the dog's house   Jill's coat   Miss Smith's car   Tom's book   a boy's boots   a cat's mat

◆Add an **apostrophe** and an **s** ('s) to show possession or ownership.

door of car	car's door	Bible of Cal	Cal's Bible
pen of Mike	Mike's pen	spoon of baby	baby's spoon
desk of Pam	Pam's desk	shoe of Judy	Judy's shoe
hat of Ted	Ted's hat	wall of room	room's wall
scarf of Jan	Jan's scarf	cup of child	child's cup
collar of dog	dog's collar	dress of lady	lady's dress

An -s is added to many words to make them **plural**.   cat cats   boy boys
The 's is added to show ownership.   cat's food   boy's balloons

◆Complete these sentences with the correct words from the box at the right.

1. The coat has four __buttons__ .   buttons   button's
2. The __boy's__ boots are under his bed.   boys   boy's
3. The __rabbit's__ food is in the box.   rabbits   rabbit's
4. My __sister's__ coat is in the closet.   sisters   sister's
5. The __tigers__ are in the jungle.   tigers   tiger's
6. Tom sat in the __dentist's__ chair.   dentists   dentist's
7. We fed each of the __kittens__   kittens   kitten's
8. We could hear the __cow's__ bell.   cows   cow's
9. Dad hammered sixteen __nails__ in the wall.   nails   nail's

---

Level C   137

The Apostrophe for Possession

Rule 1: To show that someone or something owns or possesses something, usually an **apostrophe** and **s** ('s) are added to the end of the word.   a pony's saddle   the man's hat
☆If a word needs to be plural and possessive, make the word plural, then add the 's. children's
☆If a plural word ends in **s**, usually just the **apostrophe** is added to make it possessive.
six cows' bells   many boys' jackets   three girls' dresses   five kittens' bowls

◆As you study each phrase, underline the word with the **apostrophe** and think about how many people or things have something. If one person or thing has something, print the word **one** on the line. If more than one person or thing possesses something, print **more than one** on the line.

Eric's room	one	the robin's nest	one
the babies' cribs	more than one	the eagles' wings	more than one
the lady's purse	one	the puppies' ears	more than one
the horses' barn	more than one	the cities' lights	more than one
the duck's beak	one	the radio's plug	one
the monkeys' tails	more than one	the men's tools	more than one
the men's cases	more than one	the girls' shoes	more than one

◆Add an **apostrophe** and an **s** ('s) or just an **apostrophe** (') to show possession or ownership.

1. If women have a meeting, it is the __women's meeting__ .
2. If kangaroos have a yard, it is the __kangaroos' yard__ .
3. If the babies have scarves, they are the __babies' scarves__ .
4. Alison was given a doll, so it is __Alison's doll__ .
5. The wolves have a den which is the __wolves' den__ .
6. Lonna has many toys, so they are __Lonna's toys__ .
7. Dad gave Joey a Jeep, so it is __Joey's Jeep__ .
8. Some boots belong to Connel, so they are __Connel's boots__ .
9. The bunnies live in a box, so it is the __bunnies' box__ .

Page 138

Purpose

To teach the use of an apostrophe with contractions.

Lesson

Carefully go over the rules on how to form contractions. Contractions are usually used in more informal writings, such as friendly letters, rather than in reports and other written material.

Discuss the following examples:

do not	⇨	don't
he is	⇨	he's
you will	⇨	you'll
we have	⇨	we've
was not	⇨	wasn't
they are	⇨	they're
she would	⇨	she'd

When your student has a good understanding of the page and he has given the answers orally, have him do the work independently.

Page 139

Purpose

To give additional work on the use of an apostrophe with contractions.

Lesson

Before you carefully go over the lesson with the student, discuss the following examples:

hadn't	⇨	had not
she's	⇨	she is
we'll	⇨	we will
you've	⇨	you have
isn't	⇨	is not
we're	⇨	we are
he'd	⇨	he would
(or)	⇨	he had

When he understands the page and has given the answers orally, have him do the work independently.

Note: The contraction *'d* can stand for either *would* or *had*, depending on the context in which it is used. For example, *he'd* may stand for *he would* or *he had*.

---

138   Adventures in Phonics

The Apostrophe for Contractions

A **contraction** is a short way of writing two special words. They are written together, but **one or more** letters are left out. This lesson gives the second way in which the **apostrophe** is used.
Rule 2: An **apostrophe** is used to replace the missing letters. Usually the first word is not changed.
do not = don't   they have = they've   she is = she's   you are = you're   we will = we'll

◆Print these words as **contractions**, putting in an **apostrophe** when the underlined letters are removed. do not = don't   would not = wouldn't   were not = weren't

do not	don't	should not	shouldn't	are not	aren't
had not	hadn't	were not	weren't	does not	doesn't
has not	hasn't	was not	wasn't	is not	isn't
have not	haven't	could not	couldn't	did not	didn't

◆Print these words as **contractions**. Take out the underlined letters, as in we are = we're.

they are	they're	you will	you'll	he had	he'd
you are	you're	it will	it'll	she had	she'd
we are	we're	I will	I'll	they had	they'd
we would	we'd	he will	he'll	you have	you've
he would	he'd	she will	she'll	we have	we've
she would	she'd	we will	we'll	they have	they've
they would	they'd	they will	they'll	I am	I'm

◆Complete these sentences with **contractions** made from the words in the box at the right.

1. Jim didn't get much sleep, so he can't stay awake.
2. I'm hoping that you're able to come to my party.
3. Jan knows she wouldn't be able to eat a big pizza.
4. Mother thinks that she'll go shopping today.
5. Now that this page is finished, we'll need a rest.

did not
can not
I am
you are
would not
she will
we will

Level C   139

The Apostrophe for Contractions

Review again **Rule 2:** An **apostrophe** is used to replace the missing letters in contractions. Usually the first word is not changed. An exception to the rule is will not = won't.
do not = don't   they have = they've   she is = she's   he would = he'd   we will = we'll

◆Print the two words that make up these contractions. ☆Notice: can not = can't   will not = won't

don't	do	not	couldn't	could	not
hadn't	had	not	isn't	is	not
hasn't	has	not	didn't	did	not
haven't	have	not	aren't	are	not
wasn't	was	not	doesn't	does	not
can't	can	not	won't	will	not

they're	they	are	I'm	I	am
you're	you	are	he's	he	is
we're	we	are	it's	it	is
they'll	they	will	we'd	we	would/had
you'll	you	will	he'd	he	would/had
it'll	it	will	they've	they	have
I'll	I	will	you've	you	have

◆Print the two words that make up each underlined **contraction** in the box at the right.

1. Soon we'll go out and play in the yard.
2. We wouldn't go until Mark finished his lesson.
3. He's happy that he has a new mitt.
4. It'll be fun to play catch with a baseball.
5. We're happy to have time to work and play.

we will
would not
He is
It will
We are

Page 140

Purpose
To give additional work on the use of an apostrophe with contractions.

Lesson
Discuss the rule for contractions. Where does the apostrophe belong? Does the first word get changed?

When the student understands the page and has given the answers orally, have him do the work independently.

Page 141

Purpose
To review the use of the apostrophe with possessive words and contractions.

Lesson
Go over the entire page with your student. Does he need additional work on this subject? If so, go back to the previous lessons for a review.

After he has a good understanding of the page and has given the answers orally, have him complete the work independently.

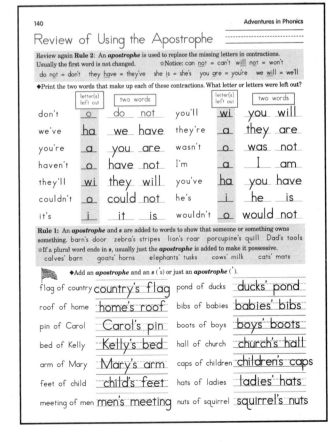

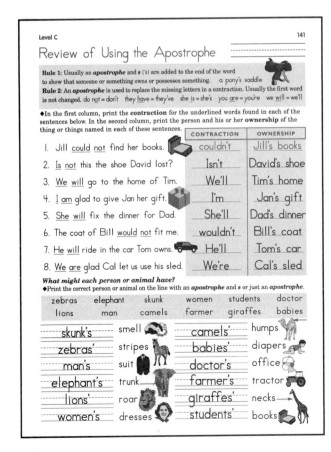

Page 142

Purpose

To become acquainted with words that have a similar meaning.

Lesson

Discuss the definition of the word synonym. Have the student give a synonym of the following words:

WORDS	SYNONYMS
happy	glad, joyful
big	large, huge
quick	fast
gift	present, toy
little	small, tiny
close	shut

After answering orally, he should be ready to do the work by himself.

Page 143

Purpose

To review words that are synonyms.

Lesson

Listen to your student as he gives the answers orally in this lesson.

When he understands the page and has given the answers orally, have him do the work independently.

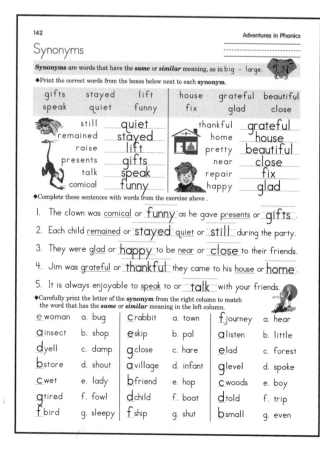

142

Adventures in Phonics

Synonyms

Synonyms are words that have the *same* or *similar* meaning, as in big – large.

◆Print the correct words from the boxes below next to each **synonym**.

gifts	stayed	lift		house	grateful	beautiful
speak	quiet	funny		fix	glad	close

still	quiet	thankful	grateful
remained	stayed	home	house
raise	lift	pretty	beautiful
presents	gifts	near	close
talk	speak	repair	fix
comical	funny	happy	glad

◆Complete these sentences with words from the exercise above.

1. The clown was comical or **funny** as he gave presents or **gifts**.

2. Each child remained or **stayed** quiet or **still** during the party.

3. They were glad or **happy** to be near or **close** to their friends.

4. Jim was grateful or **thankful** they came to his house or **home**.

5. It is always enjoyable to speak to or **talk** with your friends.

◆Carefully print the letter of the **synonym** from the right column to match the word that has the *same* or *similar* meaning in the left column.

e woman	a. bug	C rabbit	a. town	f journey	a. hear
a insect	b. shop	e skip	b. pal	a listen	b. little
d yell	c. damp	g close	c. hare	e lad	c. forest
b store	d. shout	a village	d. infant	g level	d. spoke
C wet	e. lady	b friend	e. hop	C woods	e. boy
g tired	f. fowl	d child	f. boat	d told	f. trip
f bird	g. sleepy	f ship	g. shut	b small	g. even

Level C

143

Synonyms

Synonyms are words that have the *same* or *similar* meaning, as in under – below.

◆Print the words next to the **synonyms**.

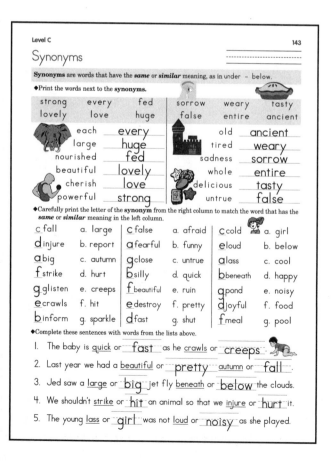

strong	every	fed		sorrow	weary	tasty
lovely	love	huge		false	entire	ancient

each	every	old	ancient
large	huge	tired	weary
nourished	fed	sadness	sorrow
beautiful	lovely	whole	entire
cherish	love	delicious	tasty
powerful	strong	untrue	false

◆Carefully print the letter of the **synonym** from the right column to match the word that has the *same* or *similar* meaning in the left column.

c fall	a. large	c false	a. afraid	C cold	a. girl
d injure	b. report	a fearful	b. funny	e loud	b. below
a big	c. autumn	g close	c. untrue	a lass	c. cool
f strike	d. hurt	b silly	d. quick	b beneath	d. happy
g glisten	e. creeps	f beautiful	e. ruin	g pond	e. noisy
e crawls	f. hit	e destroy	f. pretty	d joyful	f. food
b inform	g. sparkle	d fast	g. shut	f meal	g. pool

◆Complete these sentences with words from the lists above.

1. The baby is quick or **fast** as he crawls or **creeps**.

2. Last year we had a beautiful or **pretty** autumn or **fall**.

3. Jed saw a large or **big** jet fly beneath or **below** the clouds.

4. We shouldn't strike or **hit** an animal so that we injure or **hurt** it.

5. The young lass or **girl** was not loud or **noisy** as she played.

Page 144

Purpose
To review words that have opposite meaning.

Lesson
After discussing the directions, listen to your student give an antonym for each of the following words:

WORDS	ANTONYMS
in	out
fast	slow, poky
yes	no
good	bad, naughty
hot	cold, freezing
difficult	easy, simple

When he understands the page and has given the answers orally, have him do the work independently.

Page 145

Purpose
To review words that have opposite meaning.

Lesson
Listen to your student as he gives the answers orally in this lesson.

When he has a good understanding of the page and has given the answers orally, have him complete the work independently.

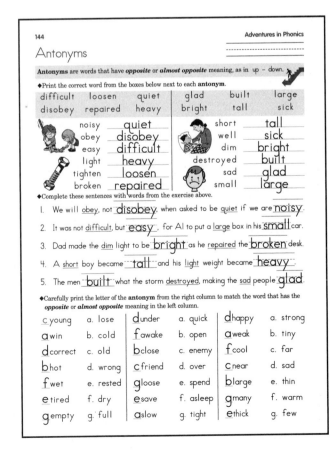

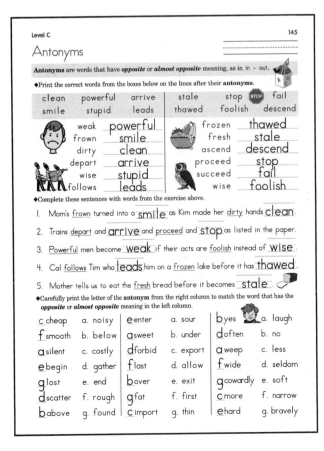

Page 146

Purpose

To have additional work with words and their meanings.

Lesson

Carefully discuss the definitions of synonyms and antonyms.

When the student understands the page and has given the answers orally, have him do the work by himself.

Page 147

Purpose

To give additional work with words and their meanings.

Lesson

Does the student know the definitions of synonyms and antonyms? Carefully discuss the lesson.

When your student has a good understanding of the page and has given the answers orally, have him do the work independently.

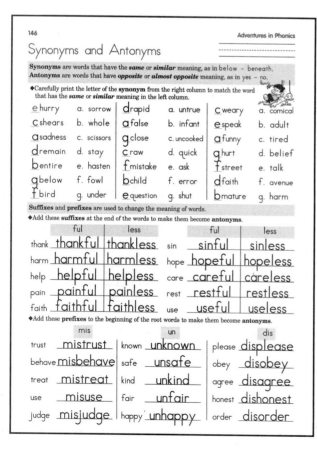

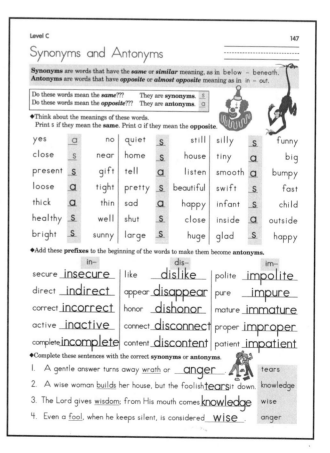

Page 148

Purpose
To help the student become familiar with words that are homonyms.

Lesson
Carefully discuss this lesson. Working with homonyms is usually enjoyable. To understand their meaning may be a little more difficult. It is important to talk about the definitions.

After discussing the directions, have your student write a homonym for each of the following words:

WORDS	HOMONYMS
do	dew, due
weak	week
one	won
threw	through
write	right
to	two, too

When your student understands the page and has given the answers orally, have him do the work independently.

Page 149

Purpose
To help the student become familiar with words that are homonyms.

Lesson
Carefully discuss this lesson. It is important to talk about the definitions.

When your student understands the page and has given the answers orally, have him do the work independently.

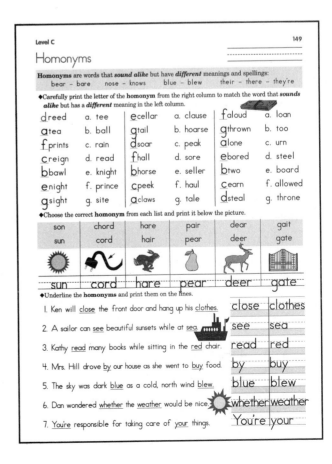

Page 150

Purpose
To help the student become familiar with words that are homonyms.

Lesson
Carefully discuss this lesson. Working with homonyms is usually enjoyable. It is important to talk about the definitions.

When your student understands the page and has given the answers orally, have him do the work independently.

Page 151

Purpose
To help the student become familiar with words that are homonyms.

Lesson
Carefully discuss this lesson. It is important to talk about the definitions.

When your student understands the page and has given the answers orally, have him do the work independently.

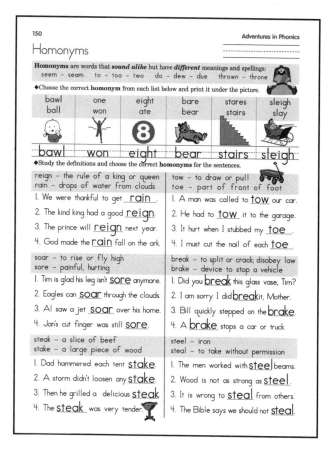

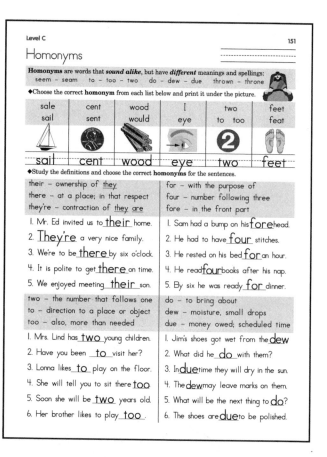

Page 152

Purpose

To help the student become familiar with words that are homonyms.

Lesson

Carefully discuss this lesson. It is important to talk about the definitions.

When your student understands the page and has given the answers orally, have him do the work independently.

Page 153

Purpose

To understand the definitions of words that are synonyms, antonyms, and homonyms.

Lesson

Carefully discuss this lesson.

When you have carefully gone over the page with your student and he has given the answers orally, have him do the work independently.

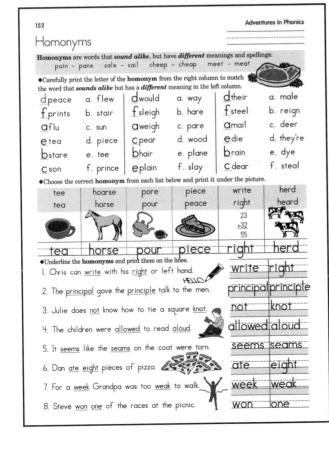

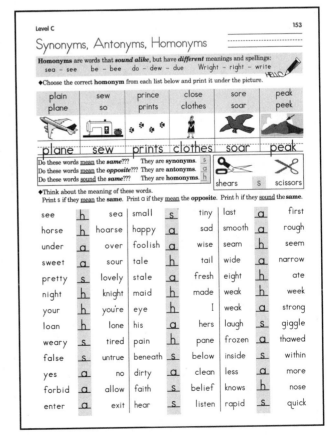

Page 154

Purpose

To review the short vowel rule.

To give more practice in using two-syllable words.

Lesson

If the student is not able to read short vowel words quickly, have him spend time reviewing **Charts 1, 2, and 3** (found on page 181 in the workbook) before discussing this lesson.

After you have carefully gone over the page with your student and he has given the answers orally, have him do the work independently.

Page 155

Purpose

To review the short vowel rule.

To give more practice in adding suffixes to short vowel words.

Lesson

Again, if the student is not able to quickly read short vowel words, have him spend time reviewing **Charts 4 and 5** (found on pages 181 and 182 in the workbook) before discussing this lesson.

When he has a good understanding of this lesson, and has given the answers orally, he may then print the answers independently.

Note: The last word (*hard*) at the bottom of page 155 is not a short vowel word, as emphasized in this lesson. Even so, *hard* should be marked as a modified **är** word.

Page 156

Purpose

To review the rule for spelling words ending with these double consonants.

Lesson

When you have carefully gone over the page with your student and he has given the answers orally, he may then print the answers independently.

Have your student read the lists of words after he has completed the written work.

Page 157

Purpose

To review rules for making words plural.

To recognize the number of syllables in words.

Lesson

Carefully review the rules for making words plural at the top of the lesson.

After you have listened to your student give the answers to the lesson orally, ask him to complete it independently.

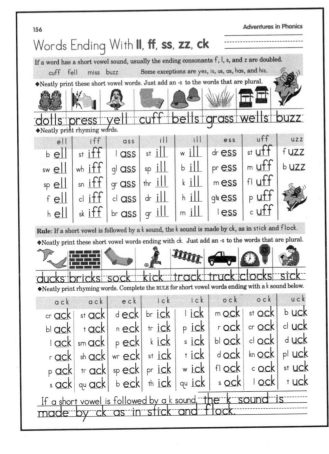

Page 158

Purpose

To give additional practice in reading words spelled with **o** having the short vowel **u** sound.

To review words spelled with **ea** that make the short vowel **e** sound.

Lesson

As you discuss this review lesson, it would be good to review **Charts 6** and **12** (found on pages 182 and 183 in the workbook).

After you have gone over the entire lesson and have heard your student give the answers orally, have him complete the page independently.

Page 159

Purpose

To give additional practice in using words ending with **nk** and **ng**.

To review compound words.

Lesson

As you discuss this review lesson, it would be good to review **Chart 23** (found on page 186 in the workbook).

When you have carefully gone over the page with your student and he has a good understanding of it, he may then print the answers independently.

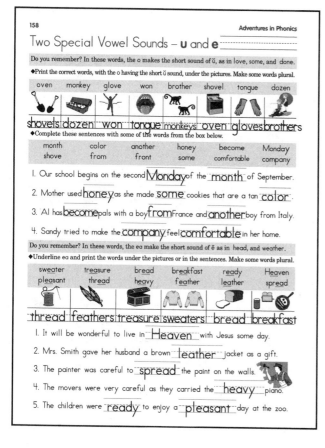

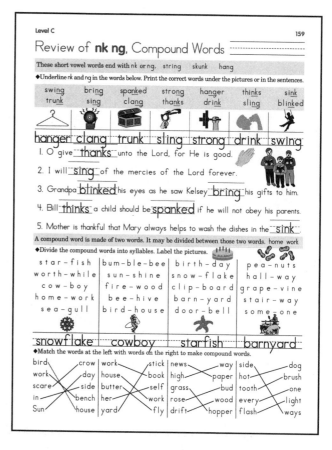

Page 160

Purpose

To review the different ways of spelling long vowel **a** words.

Lesson

After you have carefully gone over the page with your student and he has given the answers orally, he may then print the answers independently.

If you feel your student needs to have extra drill, listen to him read **Chart 10** (found on page 183 in the workbook).

Page 161

Purpose

To review the different ways of spelling long vowel **e** words.

Lesson

Before you discuss the different ways the long vowel e sound is spelled, have the student review **Chart 11** (found on page 183 in the workbook).

When you have carefully gone over the page with your student and he has a good understanding of it, he may then print the answers independently.

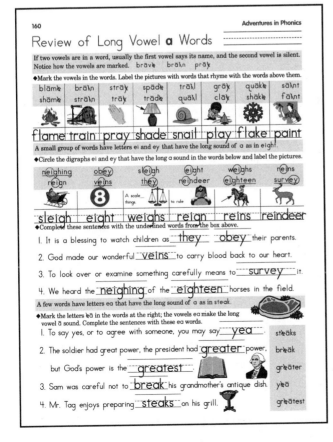

Page 162

Purpose
To review the different ways of spelling long vowel **i** words.

Lesson
Before you discuss the lesson with your student, it would be helpful to review **Charts 13, 16, and 17** (found on pages 184 and 185 in the workbook).

After you have carefully gone over the page with your student and he has a good understanding of it, he may then print the answers independently.

Page 163

Purpose
To review the different ways of spelling long vowel **o** words.

Lesson
Before you discuss the lesson, listen to your student read **Charts 14** and **18** (found on pages 184 and 185 in the workbook).

After you have gone over the page with your student and he has given the answers orally, he may then complete the answers independently.

---

162   Adventures in Phonics

Review of Long Vowel **i** Words

If two vowels are in a word, usually the first vowel says its name, and the second vowel is silent. Notice how the vowels are marked. drīve tīe sky (A y acts as a vowel at the end of words).

♦ Mark the vowels in the words. Label the pictures with words that rhyme with the words above them.

whīle	wīde	tīe	shy(ī)	fry(ī)	strīpe	tīme	fīre
pīle	sīde	dīe	try(ī)	why(ī)	wīpe	chīme	wīre
tīle	tīde	līe	spy(ī)	dry(ī)	rīpe	līme	hīre

smile   bride   pie   fly   cry   pipe   dime   tire

Usually the vowel i is short when it is alone in a word. In these words the vowel i is long because it is followed by ld, nd, or gh. The consonants gh are silent. mīld mīnd mīght

♦ Mark the ī as a long vowel. Label the pictures with words that rhyme with the words above them.

| grīnds | mīght | mīld | kīnd | brīght | bīnd |
| wīnds | sīght | wīld | remīnd | fīght | fīnd |

blinds   light   child   hind   right   mind

♦ Complete these sentences with words from the boxes above and rhyming words from the lines above.

1. May we use the wonderful __mind__ God gave us to think good thoughts.

2. Steven turned on the __light__ to make the dark room __bright__.

3. It smells good as Julie __grinds__ coffee beans to make fresh coffee.

4. Mr. Tell is __kind__ and loving to his little __child__.

5. Karen will __find__ a clean cloth to dust the __blinds__ on the windows.

♦ Divide these compound words as you have learned. Underline the words with the long i sound.

pipe–line	life–boat	fire–side	tide–water
side–walk	neck–tie	time–piece	fire–place
grind–stone	mile–post	wild–cat	blind–fold
street–light	pine–apple	white–wash	sight–seeing

Level C   163

Review of Long Vowel **o** Words

If two vowels are in a word, usually the first vowel says its name, and the second vowel is silent. Notice how the vowels are marked. hōpe fōam blōw (A w acts as a vowel at the end of words).

♦ Mark the vowels in the words. Label the pictures with words that rhyme with the words above them.

hōpe	bōat	rōw	pōse	bōast	glōw	drōve	gōad
dōpe	cōat	grōw	hōse	rōast	shōw	dōve	rōad
cōpe	mōat	thrōw	nōse	cōast	flōw	cōve	lōad

rope   goat   crow   rose   toast   snow   stove   toad

Usually the vowel o is short when it is alone in a word. In these words the vowel o is long because it is followed by ld, st, th, ll, or lt. hōld mōst bōth rōll jōlt

Mark the ō as a long vowel. Label the pictures with words that rhyme with the words above them.

| bōld | mōst | rōll | cōlts | cōlder | sōld |
| mōld | hōst | strōll | jōlts | hōlder | scōld |

hold   post   scroll   bolts   folder   old

♦ Complete these sentences with words from the boxes above and rhyming words from the lines above.

1. Jim stood next to a fence __post__ and saw his __colt__ gallop in the field.

2. When his neighbor __sold__ the colt to him, he spent __most__ of his money.

3. The men used many __bolts__ as they built the long bridge.

4. Judy had to use the rolling pin to __roll__ out the dough for the cookies.

Vowels ou can make the long vowel ō sound in some words as in bōulder.

♦ Mark the letters ōu in the words at the right and print these words in the sentences.

1. __Although__ it was big, Cal carried the bag on his __shoulder__.

2. We should love the Lord with all our heart, __soul__ and mind.

3. Missy helped her mother mix the __dough__ for the doughnuts.

| sōul |
| shōulder |
| Althōugh |
| dōugh |

Page 164

Purpose

To review the different ways of spelling long vowel **u** words.

Lesson

Before you discuss the lesson with your student, have him read **Chart 15** (found on page 184 in the workbook). Is he able to quickly read long vowel words? Does he need to review the charts again?

After you have carefully gone over the page with your student and he has given the answers orally, he may then complete the answers independently.

Page 165

Purpose

To review the different sounds made by **oo**.

Lesson

Discuss the lesson with your student. If extra review is needed, read **Charts 19** and **20** (found on page 185 in the workbook).

When you have carefully gone over the page with your student and he has given the answers orally, he may then complete the answers independently.

Page 166

Purpose

To review the many ways to spell modified vowel words.

Lesson

Carefully discuss the words in this lesson. If you feel that extra drill is needed, then review **Charts 24–27** (found on page 187 in the workbook).

After you have gone over the page with your student and he has a good understanding of it, he may complete the answers independently.

Page 167

Purpose

To give additional work with words having the sounds of **ou** and **oi**.

To review using the articles **a** and **an** with words.

Lesson

Discuss the lesson with your student. If you feel that extra drill is needed, have him read **Charts 21** and **22** (found on page 186 in the workbook).

When you have gone over the page and your student has given the answers orally, he may then complete the answers independently.

---

166   Adventures in Phonics

Review of Modified Vowels

When the consonant r comes after a vowel, it changes or modifies that vowel sound.

ar or ir er ur ear wor   are air err ear arr eir ere

◆Underline ar, or, ir, er, ur, ear, and wor in the words below and print correct words under the pictures.

soccer	carton	tornado	thermometer	worship	learning
world	rehearsal	morning	marshmallows	squirrel	search

worship   squirrel   world   learning   soccer   carton

◆Complete these sentences with words from the box above.

1. Everyday we looked at the **thermometer** to check the temperature.

2. One **morning** Ken watched a squirrel **search** for some food.

3. A violent wind with a funnel-shaped cloud is called a **tornado**

4. After the choir **rehearsal**, the students roasted **marshmallows**

There are seven spellings for the modified vowel sound of âr.
âre - care   arr - carrot   air - fair   err - berry   ear - bear   ere - there   eir - their

◆Underline are, arr, air, err, and ear in the words below and print the correct words under the pictures.

terrible	careful	berry	chairs	parrots	narrow
squares	errand	marry	dairy	beware	carrots

carrots   chairs   narrow   marry   parrots   squares   berry

◆Complete these sentences with words from the box above.

1. A **terrible** storm was to come to our area.

2. Henry was told to **beware** of the storm winds.

3. He will be **careful** as he goes home.

4. Henry has been on an **errand** for Miss Cheryl.

5. He went to the **dairy** to buy a gallon of milk.

Match the homonyms

hare — pare
merry — bear
pear — stairs
there — marry
stares — hair
bare — their

Level C   167

Review of Vowel Diphthongs **ou**, **oi**

A diphthong has **two** vowels sounded so that both vowels can be heard blended together as one. Two sets of vowels make this sound: ow is used at the **end** of words or in words **ending** with l and n; ou is usually used in other words. Remember: w is a vowel when it follows another vowel.

◆Underline the ow or ou in the words. Label the pictures with words that rhyme with the words above them.

powers towers	house blouse	frown brown	pouch crouch	trowels vowels	shout sprout

flowers   mouse   crown   couch   towels   snout

◆Complete these sentences with words from the right.

mountains   thousands   ground   fountains

1. God kept Noah and **thousands** of creatures safe on the ark.

2. God opened the **fountains** of the deep that covered the **mountains**

3. In a year the **ground** was dry as Noah's family and animals came out.

Remember! A diphthong has **two** vowels sounded so that both vowels can be heard blended together as one. Two sets of vowels make the diphthong oi sound: oi as in broil and oy as in boy.

◆Underline the oi or oy in the words. Label the pictures with words that rhyme with the words above them.

joins	oil soil	enjoys joys	spoil broil	ploys toys	joint

coins   coil   toys   foil   boys   point

Remember! 1. The word a is used before a word that begins with a **consonant**: a dinosaur.
          2. The word an is used before a word that begins with a **vowel**: an elephant.

◆Think of the RULES above as you print a or an before the names of animals that were on the ark.

a gorilla	an opossum	a squirrel	a bear	an antelope
a camel	a platypus	an otter	a cougar	an elk
an eagle	a peacock	a lemming	an alligator	a sheep
an insect	an anteater	a cow	a falcon	a hyena

Page 168

Purpose

To review the ways to spell words with the sound of ô.

To review the many sounds of **ou**.

Lesson

Before you discuss the lesson with your student, it would be good to review **Chart 30** (found on page 188 in the workbook).

After you have gone over the page with him, he may then complete the answers independently.

Page 169

Purpose

To review and work with suffixes and syllables.

Lesson

Discuss the definitions of a suffix and a syllable.

After you have carefully discussed the page with your student and he has given the answers orally, he may then complete the answers independently.

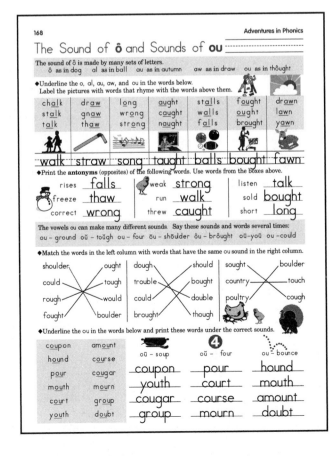

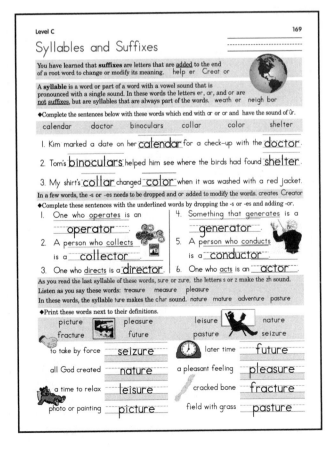

Page 170

Purpose

To review the three sounds that the suffix **-ed** makes.

To give additional review in adding suffixes.

Lesson

Carefully go over this lesson to see that your student understands how to add suffixes to root words.

When you feel he is ready, ask him to complete the page independently.

Page 171

Purpose

To have more practice in working with words ending with **y**.

Lesson

Discuss the rules of adding suffixes to words ending with **y**.

After you think he understands the lesson, ask your student to complete the page.

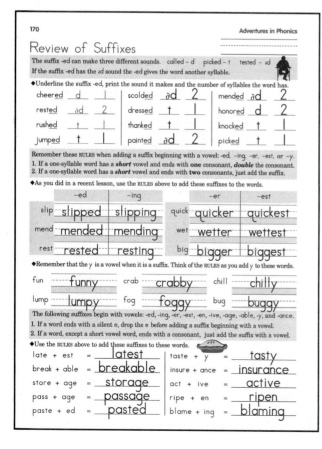

170   Adventures in Phonics

Review of Suffixes

The suffix -ed can make three different sounds. called – d   picked – t   tested – ad
If the suffix -ed has the ad sound the -ed gives the word another syllable.

◆Underline the suffix -ed, print the sound it makes and the number of syllables the word has.

cheer*ed*	d	1	scold*ed*	ad	2	mend*ed*	ad	2
rest*ed*	ad	2	dress*ed*	t	1	honor*ed*	d	2
rush*ed*	t	1	thank*ed*	t	1	knock*ed*	t	1
jump*ed*	t	1	paint*ed*	ad	2	pick*ed*	t	1

Remember these RULES when adding a suffix beginning with a vowel: -ed, -ing, -er, -est, or -y.
1. If a one-syllable word has a **short** vowel and ends with **one** consonant, **double** the consonant.
2. If a one-syllable word has a **short** vowel and ends with **two** consonants, just add the suffix.

◆As you did in a recent lesson, use the RULES above to add these suffixes to the words.

	-ed	-ing		-er	-est
slip	slipped	slipping	quick	quicker	quickest
mend	mended	mending	wet	wetter	wettest
rest	rested	resting	big	bigger	biggest

◆Remember that the y is a vowel when it is a suffix. Think of the RULES as you add y to these words.

| fun | funny | crab | crabby | chill | chilly |
| lump | lumpy | fog | foggy | bug | buggy |

The following suffixes begin with vowels: -ed, -ing, -er, -est, -en, -ive, -age, -able, -y, and -ance.
1. If a word ends with a silent e, drop the e before adding a suffix beginning with a vowel.
2. If a word, except a short vowel word, ends with a consonant, just add the suffix with a vowel.

◆Use the RULES above to add these suffixes to these words.

late + est =	latest	taste + y =	tasty
break + able =	breakable	insure + ance =	insurance
store + age =	storage	act + ive =	active
pass + age =	passage	ripe + en =	ripen
paste + ed =	pasted	blame + ing =	blaming

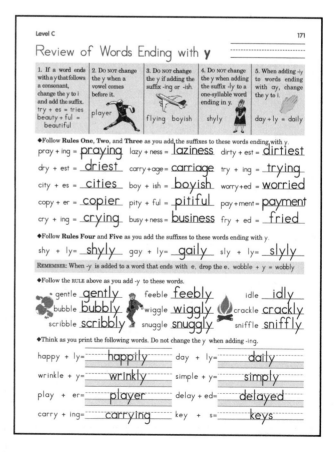

Level C   171

Review of Words Ending with y

| 1. If a word ends with a y that follows a consonant, change the y to i and add the suffix. try + es = tries beauty + ful = beautiful | 2. Do NOT change the y when a vowel comes before it. player | 3. Do NOT change the y if adding the suffix -ing or -ish. flying boyish | 4. Do NOT change the y when adding the suffix -ly to a one-syllable word ending in y. shyly | 5. When adding -ly to words ending with ay, change the y to i. day + ly = daily |

◆Follow **Rules One, Two,** and **Three** as you add the suffixes to these words ending with y.

pray + ing =	praying	lazy + ness =	laziness	dirty + est =	dirtiest
dry + est =	driest	carry + age =	carriage	try + ing =	trying
city + es =	cities	boy + ish =	boyish	worry + ed =	worried
copy + er =	copier	pity + ful =	pitiful	pay + ment =	payment
cry + ing =	crying	busy + ness =	business	fry + ed =	fried

◆Follow **Rules Four** and **Five** as you add the suffixes to these words ending with y.

| shy + ly = | shyly | gay + ly = | gaily | sly + ly = | slyly |

REMEMBER: When -y is added to a word that ends with e, drop the e. wobble + y = wobbly

◆Follow the RULE above as you add -y to these words.

gentle	gently	feeble	feebly	idle	idly
bubble	bubbly	wiggle	wiggly	crackle	crackly
scribble	scribbly	snuggle	snuggly	sniffle	sniffly

◆Think as you print the following words. Do not change the y when adding -ing.

happy + ly =	happily	day + ly =	daily
wrinkle + y =	wrinkly	simple + y =	simply
play + er =	player	delay + ed =	delayed
carry + ing =	carrying	key + s =	keys

Page 172

Purpose

To give additional review in working with words having prefixes.

Lesson

After the student has read the words in this lesson and understood how to divide them into syllables, have him carefully complete the lesson.

Page 173

Purpose

To give additional review in working with words having prefixes.

Lesson

Review the previous lesson. Discuss the meanings of the prefixes and listen to the words being read for today's lesson.

When you have gone over the entire lesson with the student and you feel he is ready, ask him to complete the written work independently.

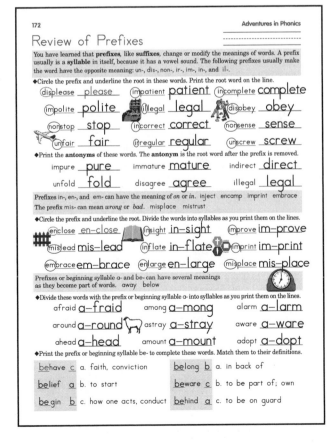

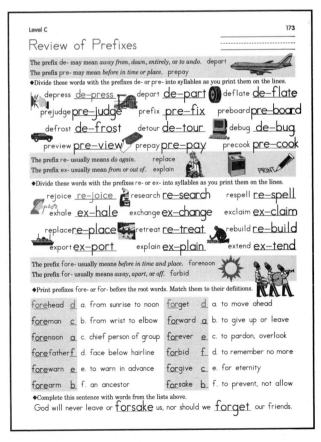

Page 174

Purpose

To review the first four rules for dividing words into syllables.

Lesson

As you discuss this lesson, ask your student to explain the rules for dividing the words.

After you have gone over the lesson and you feel he is ready, ask him to complete the written work independently.

Hopefully, you both can see an improvement in his printing.

Page 175

Purpose

To review Rules Five, Six, and Seven for dividing words into syllables.

Lesson

Have your student explain these rules for dividing the words.

When you have discussed the lesson and you feel he is ready, have him complete the written work independently.

Can he see an improvement in his printing?

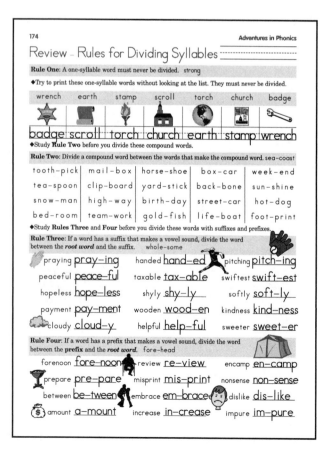

Page 176

Purpose

To review Rules Eight, Nine, and Ten for dividing words into syllables.

Lesson

After you have discussed one rule at a time, listen as your student explains each rule.

After you have gone over the lesson and you feel he understands, have him complete the written work independently.

Is he trying to be careful in his printing?

Page 177

Purpose

To have additional work with using the apostrophe.

Lesson

After you have discussed one rule at a time, listen as your student explains each rule.

When you have reviewed the lesson and you think he has a good understanding, have him complete the written work independently.

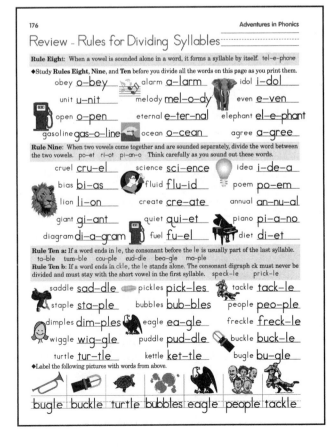

176   Adventures in Phonics

Review - Rules for Dividing Syllables

Rule Eight: When a vowel is sounded alone in a word, it forms a syllable by itself. tel-e-phone

◆Study **Rules Eight**, **Nine**, and **Ten** before you divide all the words on this page as you print them.

obey o-bey	alarm a-larm	idol i-dol
unit u-nit	melody mel-o-dy	even e-ven
open o-pen	eternal e-ter-nal	elephant el-e-phant
gasoline gas-o-line	ocean o-cean	agree a-gree

Rule Nine: When two vowels come together and are sounded separately, divide the word between the two vowels. po-et ri-ot pi-an-o Think carefully as you sound out these words.

cruel cru-el	science sci-ence	idea i-de-a
bias bi-as	fluid flu-id	poem po-em
lion li-on	create cre-ate	annual an-nu-al
giant gi-ant	quiet qui-et	piano pi-a-no
diagram di-a-gram	fuel fu-el	diet di-et

Rule Ten a: If a word ends in le, the consonant before the le is usually part of the last syllable. ta-ble tum-ble cou-ple cud-dle bea-gle ma-ple
Rule Ten b: If a word ends in ckle, the le stands alone. The consonant digraph ck must never be divided and must stay with the short vowel in the first syllable. speck-le prick-le

saddle sad-dle	pickles pick-les	tackle tack-le
staple sta-ple	bubbles bub-bles	people peo-ple
dimples dim-ples	eagle ea-gle	freckle freck-le
wiggle wig-gle	puddle pud-dle	buckle buck-le
turtle tur-tle	kettle ket-tle	bugle bu-gle

◆Label the following pictures with words from above.

| bugle | buckle | turtle | bubbles | eagle | people | tackle |

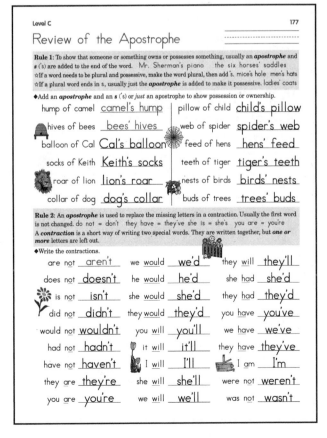

Level C   177

Review of the Apostrophe

Rule 1: To show that someone or something owns or possesses something, usually an **apostrophe** and **s** ('s) are added to the end of the word. Mr. Sherman's piano   the six horses' saddles
☆If a word needs to be plural and possessive, make the word plural, then add 's. mice's hole men's hats
☆If a plural word ends in s, usually just the **apostrophe** is added to make it possessive. ladies' coats

◆Add an **apostrophe** and an **s** ('s) or *just* an apostrophe to show possession or ownership.

hump of camel camel's hump	pillow of child child's pillow
hives of bees bees' hives	web of spider spider's web
balloon of Cal Cal's balloon	feed of hens hens' feed
socks of Keith Keith's socks	teeth of tiger tiger's teeth
roar of lion lion's roar	nests of birds birds' nests
collar of dog dog's collar	buds of trees trees' buds

Rule 2: An **apostrophe** is used to replace the missing letters in a contraction. Usually the first word is not changed. do not = don't they have = they've she is = she's you are = you're
A **contraction** is a short way of writing two special words. They are written together, but **one or more** letters are left out.

◆Write the contractions.

are not aren't	we would we'd	they will they'll
does not doesn't	he would he'd	she had she'd
is not isn't	she would she'd	they had they'd
did not didn't	they would they'd	you have you've
would not wouldn't	you will you'll	we have we've
had not hadn't	it will it'll	they have they've
have not haven't	I will I'll	I am I'm
they are they're	she will she'll	were not weren't
you are you're	we will we'll	was not wasn't

Page 178

Purpose

To give additional work with words having silent letters.

To review making words ending with **y** to be plural.

Lesson

Listen to hear your student read the words and say which letters are silent.

When you have reviewed the lesson and you think he has a good understanding, have him complete the written work independently.

Page 179

Purpose

To have additional work with words having consonant digraphs.

Lesson

Carefully review the three sounds that **ch** can make.

Listen to your student read the **gh** and **ph** words in the shaded area.

When you have reviewed the lesson and he knows the words and has given the answers orally, have your student complete the written work.

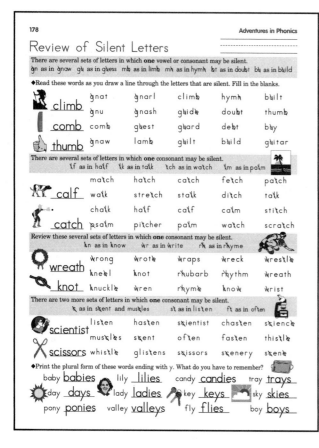

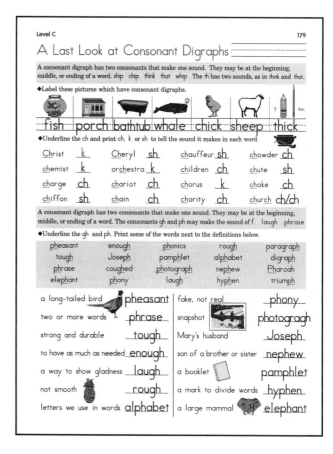

Page 180

Purpose

To have one last review of materials on some of the previous lessons.

Lesson

Carefully review this lesson as you have the other pages.

When you have reviewed the lesson and he knows the words and has given the answers orally, have him complete the written work.

Encourage and commend your student for persevering to the end of this phonics workbook. It would strengthen him to review any or all of the lessons, even on his own.

Does he think it looks difficult now that he has done the work?

Does he think he has learned much from the lessons?

May he be a better reader because he did the work.

May the Lord bless him with a desire and a love for reading.

Thank you so much, teacher, for helping your student to complete this work.

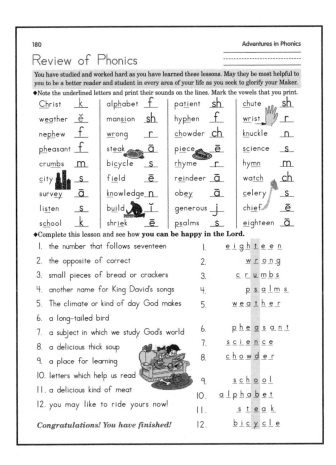